New Women's Dress for Success

ALSO BY THE AUTHOR

Dress for Success
The Woman's Dress for Success Book
Live for Success
*How to Work the Competition into the Ground
and Have Fun Doing It*
New Dress for Success

New Women's Dress for Success

John T. Molloy

WARNER BOOKS

A Time Warner Company

Warner Books, Inc., 1271 Avenue of the Americas, New York, NY 10020
Visit our Web site at /http://pathfinder.com/twep

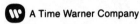 A Time Warner Company

Printed in the United States of America
First Printing: December 1996
10 9 8 7 6 5 4 3

Library of Congress Cataloging-in-Publication Data

Molloy, John T.
    New women's dress for success / John T. Molloy.
        p. cm.
    ISBN 0-446-67223-8
    1. Clothing and dress. 2. Fashion. I. Title.
TT507.M644 1996
646'.34—dc20   96-16951
                                          CIP

Cover photo by Herman Estevez
Cover design by Elaine Groh
Book design and composition by L&G McRee

This book, along with everything I do,
is dedicated to Maureen and Rob

I would like to thank Valerie Mars, whose sharp pencil and sharper mind worked with me through the book's many changes.

Contents

Foreword

A woman's success does not depend entirely or even primarily on how she dresses, but dress is an important factor in most women's careers. Research shows that when a woman dresses for success, it does not guarantee success, but if she dresses poorly or inappropriately, it almost ensures failure. Most women know men who dress horribly and are very successful. Dressing poorly does not destroy a man's career the way it does a woman's. If a man is really good at what he does, he is often referred to as "a diamond in the rough" and can move up in spite of a poor image. However, if a woman dresses inappropriately, she will be eliminated from consideration for management by most men and women managers. This is obviously a double standard and certainly not fair. However, it is the way the real world operates, and you have to deal with it.

Several months before this book was published I was challenged to prove that "dressing for success" remained a valid concept. As a result, I spent three weeks on the telephone persuading managers in 142 offices to take pictures of their people for one week. Some took the pictures with their employees' knowledge and cooperation, some took them secretly. We asked them to personally divide their employees into three categories: those who dressed for success, those who dressed suitably, and those who dressed either poorly or inappropriately. When they arrived at our office, we divided the people into similar groups based on my research. Surprisingly, even though we purposely chose thirty-four bosses who said they did not believe dressing for success was a factor in their offices, most of them placed people in the same categories we did. We then asked these same managers to place the people into three groups: those who were successful or likely to be successful, those who still had a chance at succeeding, and those who would never succeed.

Those who were thought to be good dressers by their bosses were one and a half times more likely to be placed in the top group than average dressers and almost four times more likely than poor dressers. While the numbers were not identical and our survey techniques varied, there was no substantial difference from a similar survey I conducted almost thirty years ago. It seems the more things change, the more they remain the same. Today most businesswomen still dress for failure.

When we analyzed the data we found that dress affected women, short men, and minorities more than average-height and tall white males. There were similar differences among women. It was more important for short, heavy, voluptuous, very beautiful, and older women to dress well than it was for average women. We further discovered that dress also had a greater impact on managers and professionals than on others. In fact, dressing well is a hallmark of most women managers. Women who dress poorly or inappropriately do not seem to get into management. After talking to over two thousand businesswomen in client corporations in the last three years, I estimate that within the United States several hundred thousand are qualified in every way for management but have no chance because they do not look the part. Finally, dressing professionally is most important for women who have to deal effectively with relative strangers on a regular basis. However, dressing effectively is important not only to those who must deal with strangers. Dress affects, in a meaningful way, the careers of most women, including many who think that while dressing for success may work for others, it would not work for them. A prime example of this were women scientists who worked in seven different laboratories. These women never saw or were seen by anyone but their co-workers and bosses, and some saw them only occasionally. They and their supervisors believed that all that counted was the quality of their work. Yet even in these settings, those who dressed like professionals, not backroom researchers, were twice as likely as their equally talented sisters to move into supervisory positions.

The finding that surprised the researchers was that dress counted most for those who work in casual environments. When I surveyed women managers and professionals, most of them were aware of the impact of casual dress on their ability to perform and put more effort into choosing their outfits for casual Fridays than they did for the rest of the week.

Because it was critical to the book, I ran a second study to verify the findings of the first. I located twenty-two large and midsize companies where the reviewer was required to comment on the employees' dress as a part of their annual review and talked them into participating. They became involved because they wanted to know the effect of their employees' dress on the workplace. After they received the results, seven told me that they were considering changing their dress codes.

Since each employee's perfomance was reviewed annually

or semiannually, the performance reviews gave us a view of how their dress affected their careers not only at that moment, but over a period of time. Since the purpose of the reviews is to make employees aware of their shortcomings and to motivate them to improve, often when an employee's dress was criticized, the employee changed. We ran across 102 women who were commended in the next review for their improved dress. These improvements had an interesting effect on how the reviewer, who was often the woman's immediate supervisor, saw her. In about half the cases, within two years the reviewer started looking at the woman in a more favorable light. Five to seven years later most of the remaining supervisors started seeing the women as more able, but some never changed their opinion. Apparently, when some people form an impression, they never change it. However, improving was not a waste of time. When the employees with new improved images changed jobs or bosses, their new bosses saw them, sometimes for the first time, in a positive light. This is exactly the same results we had when we trained people to be more popular. When they interacted with new people, most received the preferential treatment that all popular people receive, but when they dealt with people who knew them in the past only half responded positively to their sending popular signals.

Obviously that is bad news for people who dress poorly, but luckily it is not the whole story. A woman who starts to dress for success immediately has a measurable statistical advantage over her competitors with respect to promotions, especially when dealing with relative strangers and even when dealing with people who have known her for years. This book, which will take at most a few hours to read, can give you that advantage.

*New Women's
Dress for
Success*

Introduction

The main reason most women "dress for failure" is that when they wear an outfit their superiors think is totally inappropriate, no one tells them. Most male managers, in this politically correct age, are afraid to tell a woman she is wearing something inappropriate, and most women in management do not think it is their job.

As a result, many women make the same mistake, over and over, when dressing for work. In spite of the achievements of the women's movement, there is no "old girls' club," in which senior women go out of their way to help their younger sisters. This is unfortunate, because a substantial number of women who dress inappropriately for work have advanced degrees and enormous potential. In many ways they may be very sophisticated yet believe—since no one tells them otherwise—that they look like professionals. They have no idea that their dress is negatively affecting their careers.

This wall of silence puts these women at a tremendous disadvantage. When young men are not dressing professionally, they are often told. When I was in my twenties the vice president of my department called me into his office and told me he had good news and bad news for me. The good news was that he was making me his assistant and giving me a raise. The bad news was that he was telling me how to spend my raise. He instructed me to buy one suit and two ties a month for the next three months from his favorite salesman at Brooks Brothers. He had already told him what I needed. Each time I picked up a new suit, I reported back to my boss and he told me which of my old suits I was never to wear to work again.

Although I did not realize it at the time, advising me on professional dress was a bigger favor than giving me a promotion. I came from a blue-collar background, and I was the first in my family to go to college. It never occurred to me that I might be dressing inappropriately. I believed what most people from blue-collar backgrounds believe—that as long as I dressed decently, my dress would never hold me back.

Every year I interview hundreds of hardworking, clever, talented women who hold the same belief.

The only way to avoid this pitfall is to let research help you choose your business wardrobe.

In 1963 I conducted my first research project on clothing. I was given government money to find out if a teacher's clothing affected student performance in the classroom. After almost two years I reached a number of conclusions. The most important were these:

- While students in junior high school and high school said they liked and could relate to informally dressed teachers and would work harder for them, in fact they produced more work, and better-quality work, for conservatively dressed faculty members. When we questioned the students, we found they worked longer and harder for formally dressed teachers because they assumed they would be tough markers.

- The color and patterns of teachers' clothing affected the conduct and attention span of the students. We verified this by measuring the students' blink rate during class; the higher their blink rate the lower their concentration. After class we used standard tests to measure how much material the students remembered and understood. When we put young teachers in darker garments, they found it easier to control their classes. We also discovered that when guidance counselors wore earth tones, students were more likely to open up to them.
- There was no magic formula. While some of the larger and more intimidating male teachers were more effective when they dressed casually, most male and the overwhelming majority of female teachers were not.

My next research was conducted for law firms. They hired me to find out how young lawyers should dress to be credible with clients, judges, and juries. When I proved successful at that, they asked me to dress clients and witnesses. We discovered that if we dressed a person accused of a crime in blue with white and maroon details, they looked innocent to many jurors. In personal injury cases, clients were more likely to be believed if they wore outfits one size too large.

When these law firms found I could help people appear in a manner that increased their chances of winning cases, they recommended me to their corporate clients. I still work for many of those companies today.

At first I answered questions for corporate clients, such as Should we have a written dress code? Most of the time the answer is no. Establishing general guidelines for dress when a person is being hired is a far better idea.

What type of uniform would be best for people fixing telephones, delivering pizza, renting cars, working as tellers, driving trucks, selling real estate? We designed uniforms to send specific messages. Telephone repair workers and pizza deliverers ask people to open their front doors; therefore their uniforms must identify them at a glance. Uniforms for car rental agents and bank tellers are basically billboards advertising the company. And we designed sales uniforms to help make salespeople more authoritative, credible, and friendly.

The question asked most often was, How should our salespeople dress to sell steel, food, medical supplies, lumber, office equipment, banking services, accounting services? Salespeople sell more if they dress to match their product or service and customers.

However, by far the most challenging question was, How should I dress to sell myself? It was asked most often by two groups, college students looking for jobs and politicians doing the same.

Once people discovered that by changing how they dressed, they could improve their performance and reach their career goals, I had millions of fans—and many imitators.

Although my research reveals an evolution in how women should dress for success, my basic premise has remained the same: The job dictates the dress.

I know that the minute I mention research, most people's eyes glaze over, but without it I would be guessing, as many image consultants do. So I feel I need to talk about it briefly. Don't worry—I will not overwhelm you with reams of statistics, and I will not describe my methodology in detail.

I use standard research techniques and methods of statistical analysis. Most of the research, several million dollars' worth, is paid for by major corporations. I assure you when they spend that type of money they oversee the operation with great care. So as a researcher, I have to dot all my *i*'s and cross all my *t*'s.

While I apply standard research techniques, I do not base my advice solely on theoretical research. Whenever possible I test my findings in the real world. When I finish a study I take the results to my clients and ask if they will help me test them. Most of the time they agree, since they have invested in the results.

For example, when the research showed in 1989 that women selling important products to very conservative males were more effective when they wore suits in muted feminine colors than in traditional business colors, I approached a bank that insisted their saleswomen dress in traditional conservative suits in traditional menswear colors. I asked them to put six of the nineteen women selling banking services in more feminine suits and compare their performance with the women who did not change. When we both agreed that their sales increased, I approached seven additional companies to run similar tests. Only after knowing six of the seven had similar results did I recommend that saleswomen wear more feminine colors. I followed this up by having the women keep DFS ("Dress for Success") calendars (see page 251), and one year later I was able to recommend specific colors and shades of colors for different types of sales.

One of the strongest arguments for my research is its staying power. In 1977 I said the suit was the most effective outfit a woman could wear. In spite of the changes in businesswomen's clothing since then, that statement is still true. Where I made my mistake was in thinking women, like men, would consider wearing *only* suits. Women opted for a much more expansive look, which includes jacket outfits and conservative dresses—the only other outfits that I recommended in my original book.

Another research tool I've developed is the use of special focus groups that I call *telephone tag teams*. Early in the research for this book I realized if I wished to give valid advice on breaking through the glass ceiling, I needed to run focus groups composed of women who had made it into top management. When I tried to gather groups of powerful, successful women together for these meetings, I discovered it was almost impossible. They were not only busy and constantly changing their schedules, but were also usually separated by great distances. The solution to the problem was suggested by a V.P. in a computer company. She regularly ran meetings with her sales managers from different parts of the country using conference calling, and invited me to sit in on her next meeting. Halfway through I decided to use her conference calling system to run these focus groups.

I call these my telephone tag teams because setting up the sessions was very difficult. Most of the time, when I tried to contact one of these women, her assistant would inform me she was tied up in a meeting and ask for my number. As often as not, when she called back I would be unavailable and we would play telephone tag. Because these focus groups were so difficult to organize, I used them only when studying the problems of women at or headed for the top. If you are in either of these two very exclusive groups, I strongly recommend that every time telephone tag teams are mentioned you pay careful attention. A vice president of an insurance company said after reading the book that reading the sections on the telephone tag teams was like having a dozen aunts and sisters in top positions that you could go to for advice. She added that the information was worth its weight in gold. I hope you agree because, if my time is worth anything, it is the most expensive research I ever conducted.

I think the fact that many of the same companies that hired me more than thirty years ago remain my clients is a good indicator that my methods work. However, the endorsement I am proudest of is the more than nine thousand women who have written to me, thanking me for changing their lives. Seven out of ten letters tell the same story. These women seemingly have every qualification for success. They are educated, hardworking, dedicated, and very competent; but somehow they did not get key assignments, recognition, or promotions they thought they so richly deserved. They were convinced that as long as they dressed sensibly they were bound to move ahead.

Most started dressing for success because they were so frustrated and desperate, they would try anything. Many had put off marriage and children for the success they were sure was inevitable. To their surprise, when they started dressing for success, people in charge started to look not only at them but at their work with greater respect and started rewarding them with key assignments and promotions.

Susan, who worked in public relations for a large firm, put it very well: "I understood that the press releases I wrote had to say exactly the right thing in exactly the right way if they were to be effective. I also understood that if I put them on plain paper, nobody would read them. They had to be packaged correctly, laid out properly, and on good stock. Yet I sat at my desk, in jeans, wondering why I was not being moved into management. Before I finished the introduction of *Dress for Success*, I knew my mistake. I was dressing the company's products and services for success, but I was not myself. I made that discovery a year and a half ago, and since then I have received three promotions. . . ."

DRESSING FOR FAILURE

Many businesswomen today dress for failure. Sixty-five to 70 percent of women with college and advanced degrees dress in ways that limit their upward mobility. Many young women make critical mistakes during their first year or two at work, when companies are putting people into different tracks, and they eliminate themselves from consideration for executive or top professional positions.

Some very sophisticated women who seem to have everything going for them dress in a way that limits their success. Professional women whose taste and background should enable them to package themselves with great skill and care seem to be missing the target. Our research indicates that about 60 percent of the women aiming at top executive or professional positions hurt their chances by dressing poorly. Some of these women are so talented that in spite of the fact that they do not dress effectively, they move into important positions. Surveys of the decision makers show that no matter how successful they are, they would have moved up faster had they dressed effectively.

Most women who dress for failure fall into one of the following eight traps:

1. Allowing Your Background to Kill Your Career

The most common reason women dress for failure is that they let their background choose their wardrobe. Women who come from less sophisticated backgrounds and rely on their own taste—or the taste of most store clerks—end up looking unprofessional. Their background has conditioned them to choose particular styles and colors and to put them together in a manner that announces to most decision makers that they are not sophisticated. This is a particularly devastating flaw if a woman has a female supervisor who comes from an upper-middle-class background. Research shows that the most effective message a woman can send to her boss is that she is a socioeconomic sister. If you come from a less sophisticated background and you are not following my research, without ever realizing it you are probably sending the wrong message.

The way to overcome a limited background is to cross-shop. Decide what you need before going shopping. If you decide you need a blue, beige, or cranberry suit, dress, or scarf, shop for that item and only that item. First go to the least expensive store in town that carries business clothing and look at its beige, blue, or cranberry dresses, scarves, suits, and so on. Then go to the most expensive stores in town and look carefully at their versions of the same outfits. Pay attention to details, the shades of colors, the look and feel of the fabric, the way the garment is finished, the way it hangs, and its style. Then go to a store where you can afford to shop and find a version of the garment that looks as if it might have come from the upscale store. Buy the garment only if it looks and feels similar to the garment in the expensive store.

Start a special clothing fund that allows you to shop in the upscale stores—remember you are investing in yourself and your future earning potential! You might be saying "But I can't afford to buy upscale clothing—or even the next best alternative," but I say you can't afford not to.

If you like to shop, you can upgrade your taste in clothing quickly. Simply make a point of visiting stores at both ends of the socioeconomic scale on the same shopping trip and carefully compare similar garments. In just a few weeks most women get a feel for a more sophisticated look. You will begin instinctively to feel that some colors, patterns, and designs are more sophisticated than others.

While doing research for one company, we reviewed the annual appraisals given by women to their female subordinates. We found that if the boss came from an upper-middle-class background and the subordinate dressed in a way that projected a blue-collar background, the manager made a negative comment about her image about 70 percent of the time. In many cases the negative comment was such that it eliminated the subordinate from being considered seriously for an executive position. Unfortunately the comment stayed in her personnel file. What made it even worse is that executives almost all read the reviews of previous managers and sometimes unfairly repeat negative comments. Obviously dressing for success from the day you start with a company is very important.

2. Falling into the Fashion Trap

If you allow the fashion industry to influence what you wear to work, it's almost like letting a stranger write your résumé. Part of the message you send every day when you walk into the office is sent by what you wear. If a man wears fashionable clothing, most businessmen think he is a lightweight—not the kind of person who can be trusted with important matters. If a woman dresses fashionably, she sends the same message—and it is one that no woman with serious career ambitions can afford to send.

Keep in mind that fashion is basically a marketing tool and the people in the fashion industry are more interested in their success than yours. Fashionable clothing has been a big moneymaker, and naturally the industry puts most of its effort into marketing it. They don't want you buying a suit, jacket, or skirt that you can wear for many years. They want you to buy out-fits that you wear for one or two seasons, throw out, and replace.

The people in the fashion industry refer to their business as the "rag trade." The only thing that makes one rag better than another is profit. There is nothing immoral or illegal about that. It is a problem only for those women who have been convinced that fashion should be followed.

The main reason businesswomen should ignore fashion is that the fashion industry and their spokespeople completely ignore businesswomen. *The New York Times* comes out once a year with a special color supplement on fashion. In spite of the fact that many of their readers are working women, the newspaper has gone years without acknowledging that real women need real clothing for real jobs.

Fashion by its nature is overpriced and shoddy. I admit that some designer clothing is very well made, but it is not as well made as it should be for the price. Fashion clothing doesn't have to last for ten years because no woman is expected to wear a garment for ten years. Designers assume that the garment will date itself in a couple of years—or one season—and there is no reason for them to put the time, money, or effort into producing women's garments.

3. Following Advice of Self-Appointed Experts

The third reason women dress for failure is that they let so-called experts pick their clothing. If an expert says he is going to help you choose your business clothing, you should ask him what qualifies him to give advice. Remember, your future depends on his skill.

You must be very cautious about handing over your future

to a personal shopper. Many are good at picking clothing that looks attractive and are skilled at putting things together with panache. However, they often give poor advice to business-women because most of them have never worked in a tradi-tional business environment and many come from limited backgrounds. Personal shoppers who work for stores are up front, at least. You understand who is paying them, and you should understand whose interest they have at heart.

Surprisingly, the personal shoppers who work for stores often give better advice than some of the independent person-al shoppers. One reason may be that at least half of the so-called independent personal shoppers are being paid by their clients and the stores. They are getting what I call "quiet com-missions." The first thing you should ask any personal shopper is, Are you being paid a commission by any stores? If they say no, you should still insist on choosing where you shop.

The silliest advice is given by the color consultants. Of course the colors you wear are important, but the idea of divid-ing people into four groups, or "seasons," is not valid. Chapter 6 on how color really works should make your choices much easier.

4. Confusing Sex Appeal with Success Appeal

The fourth pitfall to dressing for success at work is wearing clothing that is too sexy or too revealing. Despite all the pro-nouncements by the feminist movement, many women—including some unsuccessful businesswomen—dress as sex objects. Sexuality certainly is part of a woman's life, and being sexually appealing is desirable. That does not change the way men and other women react to women who dress in an overtly sexy manner in the office.

Most men enjoy an attractive woman dressed in a sexy style. They make passes at them, date them, and perhaps marry them, but they seldom promote them or trust them with important assignments. The reaction of men is friendly compared with that of women. Our survey of 137 women who worked with women who dressed in a revealing manner showed that about one-third were openly hostile.

No woman should ever wear sexy clothing to work. Looking attractive and being charming are assets in business today, as long as you do not step over the line of good taste.

We ran tests on women in sexy outfits fourteen times over the past twenty years. Each time the results were the same: they were thought to be less effective by both sexes than women who dressed in a nonsexual way.

At one time I tried to lay out specifics on what was sexy and what was not. That was an impossible undertaking, since there were too many variables. We showed pictures of women dressed in a variety of garments to a cross section of business-men and -women and asked them to pick out the women who were dressed in sexy garments. Just about everyone picked the same people.

I am convinced that 99 percent of the women reading this book know when they are dressing too sexily. The only exception were miniskirts: there women saw fashion; men saw legs.

5. Miscalculating How Men Perceive Your Image

The fifth reason most of these women miss the target is that they assume if their female friends like what they wear to work, it must be universally acceptable. They do not recognize the obvious fact that men and women see clothing—and almost everything else—differently. For example, men divide all colors and garments into two types: business and nonbusiness. If you wear a nonbusiness color, they will not take you as seriously as someone wearing a business color. Men define business colors as the colors they wear to work.

It is true that women have conditioned men to think of them as effective when they wear feminine colors. For example, they have made mahogany- and rust-colored suits acceptable. However, these colors do not look as effective to men as gray, blue, and beige. There are advantages to wearing feminine colors: you are more persuasive and more appealing when dealing with both men and women. However, if you have to convince men that you are a competent, informed professional, wearing traditional menswear colors will make your job easier.

When I first started researching women's clothing I suspected there was a conspiracy. I thought that all those fashion magazines that were advising women to wear cute dresses knew they wouldn't work. I was mistaken. The truth is, most fashion magazines are run by women and are giving a woman's perspective. A woman writing in one magazine sang the virtues of a pale pink suit. She said it was a wonderful outfit to wear to work. It was conservative in cut, traditional in style, and worn with all the appropriate accessories. When I showed this picture to businesswomen, a majority thought it was an appropriate business garment. However, when I showed it to men, 93 percent said the wearer was not a serious businessperson. They eliminated the woman wearing that garment for serious consideration from almost every important position I mentioned. Male accountants didn't think she would make an effective accountant, male engineers didn't think she would be an effective engineer, male managers didn't think she would be an effective manager. Obviously this was a problem for a woman who worked with or for men.

The most obvious example for the male/female perceptions is the sexual message of the miniskirt. We showed women pictures of gray and blue suits that were very conservative in every way but skirt length, and they said that it was an appropriate business garment. Several explained that it was not outrageous or even inappropriate because the skirt was "not that short." When we showed the same picture to businessmen, over 90 percent said that they would be uncomfortable if their assistant wore the outfit to an important meeting. Several said that if their assistant wore it, they would not take her to an important meeting.

6. Dressing Too Casually

The sixth reason many sophisticated women fail is that they think they can dress as casually as their male counterparts and maintain a professional image. This is a common mistake made by women who work in male-dominated fields, such as engineering.

If a man dresses casually, he loses some of his authority. We showed pictures of a man and woman of normal height and weight with the same coloring wearing similar suits. The woman wore a skirted suit, and the man wore a traditional menswear suit. We asked a cross section of businesspeople to guess how successful they were and how good they were at their jobs. In most surveys the man had a slight edge. But the edge was very small, and it is shrinking every year. When you have both parties remove their jackets, the man wins hands down. When we show his picture to audiences, 80 to 90 percent always assume that he has a jacket somewhere. They also believe he graduated from college, was good at his job, and was an executive or professional. When we show a woman without a jacket, close to 80 percent of businesspeople assume that she did not take off her jacket. They also assume that she is not an executive or professional, but a clerk, typist, or secretary.

If you are working in a male-dominated environment with a casual dress code, you must dress more conservatively than the men to have equal or near equal authority. If the environment is so relaxed that you can't possibly wear a jacket, you must choose your garments carefully so that you are more conservative than your male co-workers. This takes skill.

7. Thinking You Are Too Successful to Follow the Rules

The seventh reason some very successful women fail is that they think because they are in management they can dress any way they want. They think they have earned the right to disregard the traditional dress code. They convince themselves that going casual is one of the privileges of success. If you look at male executives, you will see that it is not true for them, and I assure you it is not true for you.

8. Dressing to Smash the Glass Ceiling

The eighth reason women fail is that they assume the style that helped them get into middle management will take them to the top. It will not. The rules change for women the minute they head for the executive suite.

The executive suite is an upper-socioeconomic business club, and in order to get in you must wear the club uniform. The best garments for moving into the executive suite are suits in muted conservative feminine colors that scream money and class. These must be worn with expensive and upper-class accessories.

The traditional, high-authority look, which is most effective in middle management, does not work as well when a woman is headed for top management. The men in top management react positively to women who dress in a conservative, professional, and stylish manner.

ALMOST EVERYTHING HAS CHANGED

A number of major changes have affected the dress of businesswomen since the publication of the original *Woman's Dress for Success Book* in 1977. The most fundamental change is that the concept of dressing for success has been almost universally accepted. There are still members of the fashion fraternity who argue that a woman can wear anything to work, no matter how ridiculous, without it having a negative impact on her career. However, the vast majority of businesswomen no longer take such pronouncements seriously. Today the debate is not over *whether* women should dress for success, but *how* they should go about doing it.

The second change is the jacket outfit, which has evolved as the businesswoman's work uniform, similar to the male suit. Just before the final edit of this book, we approached a cross section of the American business community and showed them pictures of women wearing jackets as parts of conservative suits and feminine suits, as well as with unmatched skirts and blouses and dresses. Over 95 percent of those questioned identified women wearing these outfits as serious businesswomen, executives, or professionals. On the other hand, less than 35 percent described women without jackets in similar terms.

Third, over the last twenty years women have made substantial gains in industry. They have gone from being outsiders, or token representatives of their gender, to being an essential part of the American executive and professional work force. Women are no longer thought to be less able than men. When competing with men head-on, they are still at a disadvantage, but this can be at least partially offset by changing their image. Women are smaller, have higher voices, and often dress in less authoritative garments, which can make them appear less effective than their male counterparts. However, by carefully adjusting their presentation, women can overcome these handicaps. Successful executive women are three times more likely to dress in a serious conservative style than women with similar educational backgrounds and work experience who have not made it into the executive ranks.

Recently we asked twenty-two male managers who headed departments composed of at least 50 percent women to identify their most effective leaders, and everyone named at least one woman. In six departments women dominated the list. Twenty years ago I conducted an identical survey, and only three women were named. Younger women today do not realize the amount of effort and work that went into making them virtual equals of their male co-workers. Some think because they are accepted as professionals wearing feminine outfits that the traditional high-authority dress for success imitation male suits were unnecessary. They have no idea of the conditions that existed at the time. When women walk into an office today, no one assumes they are not serious businesspeople, because women in the 1970s and 1980s used everything they had, including conservative suits, to change the way the business world perceived them.

Twenty years ago, when I showed a picture of a woman wearing a very feminine dress, 94 percent of the men and women questioned assumed she was not an executive or professional, and almost as many said she was not serious about her career. Today over 60 percent believe that a woman, no matter how femininely dressed, could be an executive or professional, and the vast majority believe that women are serious about their careers. They are still much more likely to describe a woman in positive terms if she is wearing a jacket outfit or a suit, but no matter what a woman is wearing, she is not characterized automatically as an inferior being.

There are other women who think because many of the old barriers have been broken that getting ahead will be easy. That is not so. Women today are entering a far more competitive world than those of their mothers or older sisters. When I published the original *Woman's Dress for Success Book*, my corporate clients assured me that one of their top priorities was finding qualified women for key positions. While this is still true in professions that do not attract women—engineering, computer science, and the like—in many fields it is no longer true. Today insurance companies, law, media, public relations firms, and hundreds of other businesses have more qualified women apply for management-track positions than there are openings. We surveyed women who have been promoted over the last three years and found that 62 percent of them competed with other women who were similarly qualified.

The fourth change is that in many fields in the nineties women find themselves in a more competitive environment than their male counterparts.

In the early seventies I received a call from a corporate client. He asked me to use my contacts to help him find a woman who was an accountant, an attorney, and a corporate tax specialist and who knew something about his business. He was heading up an industry group that had formed to testify before state and federal legislative bodies in hopes of effecting tax legislation. After having been criticized on two separate occasions by female legislators for not having at least one woman in his group, he started looking. I knew only one such woman, and when I asked her if she was interested in working with the company, she said she would be if the money was right. I put the two of them together.

Two years later, when speaking to the president of the company, I found that he'd had to give her a multiple-year contract and pay her almost twice what they would have paid a man with similar qualifications. He explained she was the only qualified woman they could get on short notice. Fifteen years later I met the same woman at an industry convention and asked her if she was still working for the same company. She laughed and said, "Are you kidding? They wouldn't pay me big money for that long."

Today corporations can find dozens of qualified women without any problems. That is one of the reasons dressing for success has again become an important topic. Women understand that dressing for success is now as important to them as it is to any highly competitive man.

The final change in the past decade is that American businesswomen have redefined dressing for success. Styles and patterns that identify the wearer as a second-rater a few years ago are now standard executive attire. This is both good news and bad news.

It is good news because it gives women a greater range of clothing from which to choose and gives women options not available to their male counterparts. For example, a woman who has a problem with authority can use her clothing to overcome this problem in far more effective ways than a man. If she chooses a conservative high-authority suit, she will be looked upon as a high-authority person, particularly if the women around her are dressed in light, feminine colors. On the other hand, a man who puts on a male version of the same suit is just another fellow in a dark suit.

An even better example: small men and women who have a presence problem. When they walk into a room, people ignore them. In a group, when they try to add to the conversation, they are usually overlooked and interrupted. A man cannot put on a bright suit or a red jacket to draw attention to himself, while a petite woman can. A man working for most companies is limited to wearing a colored shirt, a bright tie, and expensive accessories. A woman, on the other hand, can wear an outfit that is eye-catching, a suit, blouse, and scarf combination that visually rivets everybody's attention and virtually cures her presence problem. When she stands up to speak, all eyes move to her.

Women's new expanded professional wardrobe, used wisely, makes clothing a far more effective business tool than anything a man can use.

The bad news is that the new expanded choices businesswomen have increase their chances of making mistakes. I initially recommended wearing suits exclusively because I was trying to make it as easy for women to dress for success as it was for men. A man does not need a great deal of skill to dress correctly: if he follows a few simple rules, he can almost be assured that he looks like a professional. The new expanded businesswomen's uniform, with its multitude of evolving colors, styles, and patterns, has turned into a sartorial labyrinth in which even tasteful, sophisticated women can lose their way.

Recently I ran six phone focus groups with top executives from different companies. Twenty-four of the participants were men, which is representative of most top management groups. When we asked them if how candidates dressed played a major part when they were seeking to fill a top spot, they said image counted but implied it was a minor consideration.

This was the same answer we received from college recruiters when we asked them how much image counted when they were hiring recent graduates and from managers when we asked the same question about people turned down for promotions. However, when we asked them to keep a list of qualified people who were turned down and the reasons for their rejection, image was given as a reason more than 40 percent of the time by college recruiters and 23 percent by managers.

If you have been turned down for a position for which you are qualified, or passed over for a promotion, this book may change your life. Read on!

Chapter One

The Jacket

The jacket has become the hallmark of the American businesswoman. Today it serves the same functions for women that the suit does for men. The jacket identifies its wearer as a serious career woman with power, authority, or potential. In our latest survey, 93 percent of businessmen and 94 percent of businesswomen, no matter what they themselves were wearing, assumed that women wearing jackets outranked women without jackets. No outfit, no matter how conservative and businesslike, announces the wearer is a competent professional as well as the jacket. A woman wearing the most conservative, businesslike dress will be seen as a professional by only 40 percent of the businesspeople she meets for the first time. If she slips on a jacket over the dress, the number of businesspeople who will assume she has power, authority, or potential will more than double.

A jacket can be worn with a wide variety of garments, and no matter what it is worn with, it adds authority and status to the wearer, making it a very effective and versatile business garment. Businesswomen usually wear jackets in one of four ways: with a matching skirt as part of a suit, with a blouse and nonmatching skirt, over a dress, and with pants and a blouse. I recommend only the first three.

When I first outlined this book, I intended to discuss all three ways of using the jacket in one chapter, because the jacket was the one essential component in the new executive uniform for women. The suit seemed to be steadily losing ground. Although the suit remains the uniform for executive and professional women in selected companies, it is no longer as important as the jacket, and it doesn't look as if it will ever become so again.

Hillary Clinton changed that. She made suit wearing important again. So I have dedicated the next chapter to the once again powerful suit, and in this chapter I will focus on jackets worn with coordinating skirts and dresses.

When I conducted my initial research in the early 1970s, women were not taken seriously unless they dressed in a conservative, tailored skirted suit in traditional male colors and patterns. At the time, both men and women treated women wearing jacket outfits more seriously than women wearing dresses or skirts and blouses, but their treatment of the women was not altered substantially by the jacket. It did not give women the authority or credibility to compete with men or with women wearing suits. The only jackets that worked, even moderately well, were not only in traditional male colors and patterns, but those cut fully enough to conceal the contour of the bust and hips. In addition, they had to be styled like men's jackets, down to the traditional lapels and buttons.

The traditional blazer jackets in conservative male colors still work, but no better than a number of other styles and colors. In the 1990s both men and women respond positively to women wearing jackets with feminine styles and colors. The jackets that create a professional image for businesswomen today come in various lengths, with and without lapels, puffed sleeves, nipped-in waists, felt collars, contrasting pockets, and so on. The wardrobes of successful and powerful women contain all these and more. However, all jackets do not work, and not all jackets or jacket outfits are equally effective. Wearing almost any jacket over a dress or skirt and blouse will make a woman appear more powerful and competent, but it won't necessarily put her on equal footing with a man or woman in a suit or a woman in a power jacket. A jacket is a wonderful garment for casual days. On those days it is more useful than on others. It adds a touch of professionalism, especially if you throw it over an inappropriate outfit. To do that, the jacket must be chosen carefully.

HISTORY OF THE JACKET

The critical years for the jacket were 1986–87. It was during those years that the attitude of men toward women wearing jackets changed dramatically. Women for several years had responded to a woman wearing a jacket as a member of America's business elite, but before 1986–87 most men did not. During those years the percentage of men who considered women wearing jackets to be effective rose from 22 percent to 83 percent. This is the most dramatic shift in opinion that I have ever run across. In less than two years the jacket—in men's minds—went from a garment that was worn by a woman who didn't know the game to being the hallmark of a professional or executive woman.

Even more surprising, the style of jacket that sent that positive message also changed dramatically. The list of jackets that could be worn by executive women went from one that was limited to masculine colors and designs to one that included almost an unlimited combination of feminine colors and designs.

Before I researched this shift, about half of the successful women in America responded to it. Suddenly these women, most of whom wore only suits to important meetings a year earlier, started wearing jacket outfits in feminine colors and designs when dealing with their bosses, meeting their most important clients, and going for job interviews. Successful women's choice of outfits for critical meetings are right on the mark about two-thirds of the time.

A survey I conducted for a client corporation in connection with designing a new uniform in March 1984 showed that only women wearing the traditional, conservative jackets were considered effectively and conservatively dressed by two-thirds of the male executives. By October 1987 women wearing jackets in a wide variety of colors and styles were identified as effective and appropriately attired by many of the same male executives.

I can't explain the change, because at the time the fashion industry was not pushing jackets. Yet successful women were buying them in significantly greater numbers than they had in the two previous years. My guess is that men became accustomed to seeing successful, powerful women they respected wearing jackets and started reacting positively to women wearing them, and the women noticed the change in attitude.

If over three hundred wardrobe calendars recorded in 1987 had not shown executives as equals, I would not have believed such a dramatic shift was possible.

THE RESEARCH

We ran a field study on the effect of wearing jackets in the offices of several clients. Women wearing dresses, skirt-and-blouse outfits, and pants-and-blouse outfits were sent to other departments during the lunch hour. We made sure the people who ran those departments were out or unavailable. They explained to the employees who remained at their desks that an emergency had arisen and they needed their cooperation. They told them to immediately get files and or information. They went to the person who they were told ahead of time was in charge and said, "I need the Smith files" or whatever. Their requests were always reasonable because the managers in each department helped us formulate the request. The requests were designed to take thirty minutes for one person to fulfill. As soon as the employee understood the request, the woman conducting the test said she had to return to her department and requested that the minute the files or information was obtained, they should "send it to her." Then the tester put a jacket over whatever she was wearing and went to another department and repeated her performance.

Over a period of eighteen months, 167 women in twenty-three companies made such requests. They dealt with men about half the time. Although the primary factor affecting how quickly the material was delivered was not the jacket but the personalities of the women, the requested material was delivered to the women wearing jackets 32 percent quicker. In nineteen cases the people to whom the request was made did not act on it until their boss returned from lunch. I am not sure why, but only three of the nineteen who refused to do anything were men. While putting on a jacket helped every group, women over forty years old, large women, and women wearing conservative dresses were helped least. Young women, petite women, voluptuous women, casually dressed women, and women wearing pants were helped most.

When we went back and questioned those who were asked to perform these tasks, the importance of the jacket was evident. In 61 percent of the cases they thought the woman wearing a jacket held a higher position and made a higher salary than theirs. They made no such assumption about women without jackets. This number who assumed that the jacket wearers outranked them would have been higher, but at least twenty-six women had hairstyle, makeup, or verbal patterns that identified them as lower class and the jacket only had a marginal effect on how their request was treated. A number of the clerical workers said they thought the women were speaking for their bosses or they would have ignored them. This and similar studies showed that in the vast majority of cases, throwing on a jacket instantly added to the wearer's authority, status, and, as a result, their ability to get things done.

Once I saw that businessmen had accepted the jacket as a female substitute for the male suit, I immediately started researching the effectiveness of jackets in the most common colors and styles. There are so many variables that half of the research I conducted during the last six years dealt with the jacket.

In September and October of 1987, for the first time, almost everyone we asked thought that a woman wearing a jacket over a fairly conservative outfit was appropriately attired for business. The DFS calendars confirmed these findings. They showed that many successful and sophisticated women who formerly wore only suits to important meetings were now wearing jacket outfits. By December of 1987, 63 percent of the managers and executives were wearing jacket outfits when they attended important meetings. The jackets these saleswomen, executives, and professionals were wearing were brighter and more feminine than those they had worn a year earlier. In addition, where similar jackets a year earlier elicited a negative response from most male executives and professionals, by the end of 1987 they elicited positive responses from the same men. Once the Dress for Success calendars convinced me that the jacket was being used by women as a business uniform, I knew I had to validate my findings. I chose the twin test as my first step because it is very reliable and generated hard numbers. I put together a series of photographs and videos of women wearing a half dozen different suits and a variety of jacket outfits and tested them against each other. We told the respondents that both twins were attorneys, accountants, saleswomen, managers, and so forth and asked questions such as which one was the most effective or career minded. When the responses were statistically meaningful, I surmised, since the pictures were of the same women in different outfits, that jackets had a significant impact on the way people perceived the wearer.

My researchers discovered not only that jackets worked, but that different jacket outfits sent different messages on different women in different situations. For example, when a woman wears a jacket in earth tones, most people think she is friendlier, more cooperative, and easier to work with than when she wears a gray or dark blue jacket. However, when a woman wears a navy or gray jacket, most people think she has more authority and is more of a professional than when she is wearing a jacket in earth tones. It is not surprising that both men and women should react to a person wearing a blue or gray jacket as a professional—men wearing blue or gray suits have conditioned us to respond to a person wearing blue or gray as an authority figure.

Since it is impossible to test every garment that could be worn with even the most popular jackets, I tried to identify predictable patterns. This was difficult since women in different fields need different looks. For example, we found women working as engineers and in other male-dominated fields had problems being taken seriously, and an outfit's ability to help them overcome this problem was their main criterion for judging its effectiveness. Women in sales rated outfits by how well they sold while wearing them. We had some success identifying general principles—for example, that women in darker jackets were more commanding, while women in lighter jackets were less threatening and more likable.

All of our findings were not that clear; in fact, sometimes the results were misleading. For example, in 1990, when we showed photographs of women in black jackets to men, three-quarters told us that they were turned off by the women. Had I taken this survey at face value, I would have advised women not to wear black jackets. However, when I tried to use that year's calendars to validate this finding, I found that 81 percent of the women reported that men treated them well when they wore black jackets. When we ran videos of women wearing black jackets for focus groups, we found out why. A majority of the men were turned off when we showed them a picture of a woman wearing a black jacket, but if her movements, voice, or approach was feminine, they immediately changed their minds. Black jackets work for over 90 percent of women we tested—only those who seemed hard or masculine should avoid them.

We also discovered that when women wore nonmatching jackets, they advanced in companies where there were a large number of women managers faster than women wearing suits. In companies dominated by women wearing suits, suit wearers had an advantage over a woman who wore jacket outfits. In most other companies nonmatching jackets and suits worked equally well. In very conservative companies where the women wore both suits and nonmatching jackets, suits worked best for important meetings.

We not only tested jackets against suits and dresses, we also tested jacket outfits against each other to see which ones were more effective on different women. We discovered, for example, that if a petite woman wore a bright red jacket, a gray skirt, and a white blouse, she was more effective than when she wore a solid gray suit. Apparently petite women in gray suits find it difficult to be noticed or listened to. Red jackets work best because they are vivid and call attention to the wearer, and because red is a strong color, it doesn't take away from her power. However, if you take the same bright jacket and put it on a very tall woman, it puts off most men. She comes on too strong or pushy, and they object to her.

We also conducted uniform research in which jackets were a central component. This was particularly useful because it enabled me to test variations of the same color. Often companies have a color that must be used in their uniforms, but they are willing to play with the shade of color if it will improve the effectiveness of their employees or help their image. This allowed me to test seven shades of red, half a dozen shades of navy, and over a dozen shades of gray to see if there was any difference in reaction to them. In most cases there was not.

When I had an option I tested the most popular jackets. Common sense was my guide when deciding which jackets to test. Since approximately one in three businesswomen owns a black jacket while very few women own pure white jackets, I spent more time researching black jackets than white jackets. Most of the women we surveyed not only owned red jackets, but wore them regularly and thought they were very effective.

So I tested red jackets extensively. Because the word women use most often when describing how they felt in their red jacket was "powerful," I checked to see if they were right. Women told me that they were less likely to buy a maroon jacket if they already owned a red one, so I tested maroon jackets against red jackets. Maroon jackets tested far better.

COLORS

Since no one ever wears a jacket alone, I researched jackets worn with skirts and blouses and dresses. The following list reflects this research.

Black

Black jackets work best with low-contrast skirts and high-contrast blouses. The best skirts, in descending order, are medium gray, light gray, burgundy, rust, maroon, taupe, grayish beige, charcoal gray, medium blue, and powder blue.

The best blouses in descending order are white, off white, pale blue, light beige, pale pink, red, oyster, light gray, and end-on-end blue. "End on end" is a men's shirting material, usually blue with white threads running through it. It is often found in men's button-down shirts.

If you are wearing a pink, rose, bright yellow, stark white, or any other bright skirt, a black jacket will calm it down and add a seriousness to the outfit; however, the outfit will not be very effective. A black jacket can also draw attention to the brightness and inappropriateness of the skirt. In fact, a black jacket worn with a white skirt, while aesthetically pleasing, sends the message, especially to men, that the wearer is not a serious businessperson. A majority of men see women wearing black jackets and white skirts as fashionable and chic—but not very professional.

The best dresses to be worn with black jackets, in descending order of their effectiveness, are beige with a grayish tint, light gray, pale blue, medium gray, oyster, and maroon. Try for shades that show definite but not stark contrast.

Black jackets can be used in other ways—for example, to threaten, intimidate, or show strength. That is why they are not recommended for women who for any reason intimidate people unless, of course, that is the intention. However, if you wish to intimidate people, wear a black jacket over a black dress or gray skirt and a black blouse. Do not put a solid black blouse or dress under a solid black jacket. Find one with a texture or a small print.

If you find yourself wearing a too feminine or too cute dress or skirt outfit, throwing a black jacket over it will help. Avoid black jackets that are made of shiny material or have eye-catching buttons or any other playful characteristics such as a velvet collar or puffed sleeves. Strangely, these playful touches often turn a black jacket from a business outfit to dressy evening wear, making it inappropriate for the office.

Petite women can wear bright blouses or dresses under a black jacket if they find they are ignored and wish to draw attention to themselves. It will lend a sense of presence. People will only notice you if the blouse is eye-catching.

White

White jackets work only in the summer, in the Sun Belt, and in California, where winter white has always been popular. White jackets work best when there is high contrast with the skirt and low contrast with the blouse.

Unless you already own one, don't buy one. Beige is a far better choice. White has only one advantage: it goes with almost everything.

Navy

If you are going to keep a jacket around to throw on when an important client or the boss shows up, navy is the best choice. Navy has almost as much authority as black, while sending a friendly, less threatening message. A navy blazer can be thrown on over almost anything and still work. Unlike black, when put over a very bright blouse or dress, it does not make the problem worse. Navy blue jackets calm down almost everything and make an outfit more businesslike. If you own only one jacket, it should be navy.

The skirts that tested best with navy jackets are, in descending order, beige with a gray tint, medium gray, charcoal gray, medium blue, taupe, light gray, beige, camel, and bluish gray. (This list could be much longer since navy works with so many colors.)

The best blouses with navy jackets are white, pale blue, beige, maroon, white on white, rust, ecru, end-on-end blue, pale pink, light gray, and red. While we tested mainly solid blouses with the most popular colors (such as navy), we also tested prints and found that small prints did not change the message. The best material for blouses is cotton, followed by silk, but artificial fibers work as well if they look rich.

The best dresses with a navy jacket are beige, beige with a hint of gray, pale blue, medium blue, light gray, medium gray, pale yellow, pale pink, maroon, rust, red, and pale pink.

A navy jacket with a dark skirt and blouse can be very intimidating. The same jacket worn with a beige skirt and a light blue blouse sends the message that the wearer is upper middle class, because beige and blue is an upper-middle-class combination—it says "trustworthy and traditional." If you substitute a light gray skirt for a beige one, the message remains the same. If you wear a medium or dark gray skirt the outfit becomes very authoritative.

When describing shades of color using traditional terms—for example, light, medium and dark—proved inadequate, I have used a one to ten system, with one indicating the lightest shade and ten the darkest. I have found when discussing colors that giving them a numerical value enables most people to see them more accurately.

If you must gain the cooperation of co-workers, superiors, or customers, a no. 7 blue jacket is ideal. We tested many shades of blue and found that a lighter navy worked best. Royal blue, cobalt, and other shades that had more vibrancy worked better when they were a few shades darker. On a woman no. 7 sends a friendlier message than a standard navy blazer yet is almost as authoritative.

The skirts that tested best are beige, medium gray, nos. 3 and 4 gray, beige with a gray tint, taupe, camel, no. 4 blue, and charcoal gray. Once again the list could be much longer because this jacket works with most colors.

The best blouses, in descending order, are pale blue, end-on-end blue, white, light beige, beige with a tint of gray, rust, pale yellow, maroon, red, and ecru.

The best dresses are beige, rust, maroon, creamy beige, medium gray, no. 3 gray, tan, grayish beige, red, ecru, off white, pale yellow, and grayish blue.

Medium Blue

The medium blue jacket is friendly and professional but not authoritative with men. It is a good jacket if you are a salesperson selling to men or women, but it is not a great jacket for a confrontation or for negotiations. It would be ideal to wear on a day when you have to talk your co-workers into going along with a plan you proposed. A medium blue jacket would also be an excellent choice for a woman reporter interviewing a businessman. It would announce that the wearer is a businessperson like him, without being threatening. It is a good everyday jacket, you will get along with everyone, but it is not a particularly powerful jacket. Most women think of blue as a power color, but medium blue really is not.

The skirts that tested best with medium blue are beige, dark gray, medium gray, beige with a gray tint, taupe, camel, no. 4 blue, and charcoal gray, as well as navy. In order for navy to work, the medium range has to be far enough away from it so that it doesn't look like a mismatch.

The best blouses, in descending order, are white, pale blue, end-on-end blue, beige with a gray tint, creamy beige, rust, pale yellow, maroon, red, and ecru.

The best dresses are beige, rust, maroon, creamy beige, medium gray, no. 3 gray, grayish beige, red, ecru, and pale yellow.

Light Blue

Light blue jackets are very tricky. I suggest that unless you live in a southern climate, avoid them. If you are going to wear them, however, you must wear them with darker skirts or dresses. Occasionally you can wear a contrasting blouse with them, but do not wear them at any time you have to give orders or exert your authority.

The skirts that tested well with light blue jackets are navy, medium blue, charcoal gray, maroon, and dark blue gray.

The best blouses, in descending order, are beige with a tint of gray, rust, maroon, and raspberry.

The best dresses are rust, maroon, dark gray, and dark blue gray.

Dark Gray

For most women I do not recommend gray jackets. They always look like stray suit jackets, unless they have metal buttons or some other sign that they are a sports jacket. When we showed pictures of women wearing gray jackets, most respondents assumed that the jacket was borrowed from a suit and the woman was not a very good dresser. I know you can do that with other jackets, but it somehow doesn't work with gray.

In addition, gray jackets are not flattering on most women. It gives many a washed-out, sickly look. For some reason the same shade of gray in a suit does not have the same effect. Because so many women own gray jackets, I developed a small list of garments that tested well and were flattering.

The skirts that tested best, in descending order, were medium-range blue, light blue, beige with a touch of gray in it, taupe, and cinnamon.

The blouses that tested best were white, light blue, salmon, khaki, oyster white, and ivory.

The dresses that tested best with them were light blue, khaki, and ivory.

You can wear a dark gray jacket with almost any dress or blouse combination. It will add authority and tone it down. For example, dark gray jackets dramatically increase the effectiveness of women wearing rust and maroon dresses.

Medium Gray

If you are going to wear a gray jacket, a medium gray should be your choice.

The skirts that worked best, in descending order of their effectiveness, were charcoal gray, navy blue, beige with a touch of gray in it, taupe, black, and very deep maroon.

The blouses that tested best were white, light blue, oyster, ivory, maroon, red, salmon, and twenty more colors I could list that work with medium gray jackets.

Light Gray

Light gray jackets should not be worn by most businesswomen. It is ironic that while light gray suits test as upper class and I therefore advise attorneys not to wear them before juries, light gray jacket outfits often send lower-class signals. Putting a light gray jacket over any skirt, including a black one, doesn't work, particularly if you have fair skin. Women with dark skin can wear light gray jackets, but there are so many better choices that I don't know why they would.

Beige with a Gray Tint

If you buy one lightweight jacket, this should be it. If you need only one summer jacket, this should be it. If there is only one light-colored jacket in your entire wardrobe, this should be it. It is effective with both men and women and sends positive messages to all socioeconomic groups. It announces to everyone that you are professional, competent, upper class, and a nice person. It is a color that makes you likable and works well in sales.

The skirts that work, in descending order of their effectiveness, are navy blue, medium-range blue, dark gray, black, medium-range gray, maroon, cranberry, dark brown, and brown with a touch of gray.

The blouses that work best, in descending order, are pale blue, end-on-end blue, rust, maroon, red, ecru, and light blue. So many blouses tested well that I could add another dozen without any difficulty. If you own skirts and blouses and they look good with this type of beige jacket, continue to wear them. This jacket goes with almost everything. As long as it is tasteful, it works.

Very Dark Brown

Very dark brown jackets work best with beige, khaki, and taupe skirts.

The blouses that work best are ecru, white, pale blue, and pale yellow.

The dresses that work best in descending order are beige, taupe, pale blue, and pale yellow.

However, I do not recommend dark brown jackets because they are not very effective.

Medium Brown

Medium brown jackets are highly recommended. They send a very positive message about the wearer; they say friendly and easy to get along with. It is an excellent choice for reporters and ministers. I recommend them for women in psychology and psychiatry and other helping professions. They relax people and open them up. Medium brown jackets work if they are made of wool or look as if they are made of wool in traditional suiting material. They work even better in tweed or herringbone, as long as they look soft, rich, upper middle class, and traditional.

Medium brown is the jacket of choice for the woman in the advice-giving business. It says, "Relax, you can trust me." It is not very effective for saleswomen or managers, but it is a wonderful jacket for someone in a helping trade—social workers, counselors, and so forth. It would also be effective on a person accused of a particularly unpleasant crime, and we found it worked on lawyers who were trying to become friends with the jury.

I discovered how effective this jacket was when three female ministers asked if I could come up with a uniform they could use when giving advice to people. They said that somehow the traditional robe they wore when they were preaching on Sunday, which gave them so much authority, did not work. The outfit that tested best was a medium-range brown tweed jacket. The minute they put it on, the reaction of everyone they met was positive and trusting. Every time I've tested it in similar situations, it has worked equally well.

With a medium-range brown jacket, the skirts that work best are dark brown, khaki, beige, and, if the shade of brown and blue are right, medium-range blue.

The blouses that work best with this jacket, in the order of their effectiveness, are pale blue, end-on-end blue, ecru, off white, khaki, beige, and pale yellow. The blue blouses with this medium-range brown jacket gave women counselors their most effective image.

Maroon and Rust

Maroon and rust jackets have not been standardized to the point that I can recommend skirts and blouses. We found that while one maroon jacket worked beautifully with a black skirt, another one didn't. It's a matter of taste. If you put skirts and blouses with them that are aesthetically suitable, they will probably work. If you have any difficulty matching colors, don't buy a maroon jacket.

But if you do, here are a couple of basic rules. Always wear a lighter blouse under the jacket. Very dark blouses don't work well under maroon jackets. Black and gray tested poorly. Even when they were aesthetically pleasing, they did not say professional.

Your skirt should be lighter than your jacket. Once again, black and dark gray skirts did not work. Medium-range gray and light gray skirts tested well.

Green

The only green jacket that works is forest green. However, the catch is that there are a number of shades called forest green, and each demands different skirts and blouses.

With a forest green jacket you can wear almost any skirt or blouse that is lighter, as long as it doesn't clash. Medium-range and light greens in jackets and blouses create a major image problem for about half the women who wear them. They make the wearer look sickly, less energetic, and less friendly.

If you are going to wear a green jacket, I strongly recommend forest green.

Red

Red jackets, in my opinion, are the most interesting. Originally red jackets did not test well. After Nancy Reagan wore a red suit at her husband's inauguration, red became a very popular color. By the time the Clintons were in the White House, many of the women from the new administration who appeared before Congress wore red jackets. In the intervening twelve years since Nancy Reagan made it popular, the red jacket became a very effective authority symbol.

Before Nancy Reagan made red a popular color in the 1980s, women who wore red jackets to work were looked upon by most men as being clowns. There was no question, the red jacket was a flag of failure. The red jacket became effective because so many effective women wore it, and men began to respond to it differently. This is why you don't want to be a leader in fashion or the first in your office to wear something new. When a garment is first introduced the chances are good that it will negatively affect your image.

What makes this worse is that the negative impression can remain even after the reason for it has disappeared. The executives in the company may think of you as a lightweight or ineffective, even when they begin to think of the woman wearing the new look as being very effective.

After the red jacket became an effective garment, some women started wearing red jackets that resembled riding jackets. When we first tested women wearing them, they were seen as trendy and ineffective. By 1993 it had become a standard executive garment, especially in the cities like New York or Los Angeles that are on the cutting edge of fashion.

The only skirts that work with red jackets are black, dark gray, medium gray, and navy blue.

BUSINESS BLOUSE STYLES

Neckline too low

Ideal neckline

Too dressy

Lowest acceptable neckline

Too frilly

Acceptable nonfrilly style

Tested poorly (too busty)

Tested well

The blouses that work with red jackets tend to tone down the red—white, pale blue, black, medium blue, dark gray, medium gray, light blue, and bluish gray.

Tweeds

Tweed jackets generally come in blue, gray, blue gray, and medium-range brown. The blue, gray, and blue gray tweed jackets are very effective on women in northern climates if they are worn with appropriate skirts and blouses. Tweeds from medium-range blue and gray to dark blue and gray tested best.

Tweed jackets are wonderful because they say the wearer is effective, friendly, and upper class. Their only drawback is that they are not high-authority jackets when dealing with men. Men tend to view them as sports jackets. If you are engaging in serious negotiations or confrontations with men, do not wear a tweed jacket.

In earth tones, tweeds work wonderfully for counselors and attorneys addressing jurors.

All Other Jackets

The jackets just listed are mainly in traditional male colors, because they tested best. Women can wear a wide range of colors. Raspberry, maroon, pale yellow, pale green, and creamy beige all have tested well. We also tried to test mahogany, amber, plum, and dozens of feminine colors. We limited our testing because even though the muted versions of these colors generally worked, they did not work as well as the traditional colors. Another reason for not doing further testing is that one company's plum was different from another's. So in essence there could be no agreement on which term matched which shade.

The Jacket

Almost any jacket put over a dress adds to the authority of the wearer. The only time this rule does not apply consistently is when you wear a light-colored jacket over a dark, conservative high-authority dress. A pastel-colored jacket, or one with a very feminine design, can make the dress less effective.

In well over 90 percent of cases, a jacket is the emblem of authority and professionalism. Most jackets scream "professional" to both men and women. A businesswoman who does not wear jackets in the office should keep one on hand so she can throw it on in an emergency. Successful women we interviewed said it was a lifesaver—or, at least, a career saver. Over two dozen women told virtually the same story. On a day when they were dressed poorly, they had to attend an impromptu meeting that turned out to be one of the most important meetings of their lives. Fortunately they had a jacket they could throw over what they were wearing, and they think it made a critical difference.

Suit Jackets

Many jackets that are very effective when worn with a matching skirt do not work when worn alone. The most obvious ones are pastel jackets. While women in pale yellow, pale green, and creamy beige suits are not high-authority figures, they are looked upon as competent professionals by 98 percent of women and a vast majority of men in most industries.

In addition, suits with very strong patterns—chalk stripes, oversize herringbones, strong plaids, windowpanes, or unusual designs—can send a strong but positive message. However, if you put these same jackets with a nonmatching skirt or over a dress, in a vast majority of cases they send strong negative messages. The same is true of short jackets and jackets with puffy sleeves. A woman in a suit with a short jacket or with a puffy-sleeved jacket can still be identified as a professional. She is not going to be looked upon as effective as a woman wearing a traditional suit, but she can get by. If you take one of these jackets and put it with a contrasting skirt, you will be thought of by most men and a substantial percentage of women as ineffective and second-rate.

On the other hand, really loud jackets like bright red, orange, cranberry, and fuchsia can sometimes be worn with a very conservative skirt or a dark blouse and send a positive message. But worn with a matching skirt, they are too strong and aggressive and do not work.

One of the things to keep in mind when you are buying a suit is that its jacket may have a double function. Of course, you can choose to buy a suit with a jacket that cannot be worn independently, but you should understand that a suit with a jacket that performs a double function may be a better buy.

Purple, Mustard, and Gold

Although purple, mustard, and gold jackets are very popular, they are tricky and I advise against wearing them. You can get away with muted plum and similar colors with purple shading, but not with purple. Even muted shades work only as suits, not as a nonmatching jacket. If you own a mustard or gold jacket, I strongly suggest you do not wear it to work.

MATERIALS

Jackets, like suits, should be made of wool or look as if they are. You will find wonderful jackets made of linen and of silk.

The Jacket

A woman's jacket can be made of almost any material if it looks rich. However, if the material or workmanship looks cheap, it destroys the positive message most jackets send. If you wear an obvious polyester jacket, you become a polyester peasant.

If you are a big woman with natural authority or a tall thin woman, you can get away with an unstructured jacket as long as it looks rich. However, a wrinkled jacket must look stylish. If you wear a wrinkled jacket that looks unkempt, you will kill your professional image. That is why I strongly advise against linen jackets: after a few hours the wearer looks like an unmade bed. Before you buy a jacket give it the squeeze test. Grab the sleeve in your hand and hold it for at least ten seconds. If the wrinkles do not disappear immediately, pass it by.

The primary reason nonmatching jackets work so well is that they send the message that the wearer is a serious businessperson. They do this by being serious. Anything that takes away from this serious message—color, style, accessories, and so on—defeats its purpose. The second reason jackets are so effective is that they send a nonsexual message. To be effective, jackets no longer have to conceal a woman's figure; however, the most effective ones hang ten inches below the waist and downplay the wearer's sexuality. While announcing the freedom the jacket gives women, I must at the same time note that the more things change, the more they remain the same.

Chapter Two

The Suit

In spite of the fashion industry's attempts to kill the conservative business suit, it remains a staple in most businesswomen's wardrobes. In fact, the suit made a resurgence in its popularity when Hillary Clinton became the first professional career woman to become First Lady.

However, even when the suit's popularity was at its lowest ebb around 1989, successful women continued to wear suits. At the time, my researchers asked 463 successful businesswomen who said they did not like to wear suits, "If you were going to the most important meeting of your life, what would you wear?" Fifty-seven percent replied, "A suit." When we asked them why they chose the suit, an overwhelming majority responded, "It works."

Most businesswomen do not relegate the suit to the back of the closet, to be pulled out in emergencies. Sixty-three percent of the 1,212 women managers we surveyed said they wore a suit at least once a week.

Another reason the suit remains an essential component in the new expanded uniform for businesswomen is that it has helped so many women to succeed. In 1978, a year after *The Woman's Dress for Success Book* was published, I received twenty letters a week from women saying that wearing suits had changed their lives.

Since then thousands of women have told me that before they started wearing suits they weren't taken seriously, promoted, or given a chance at major assignments, but all of that changed once they started wearing suits.

Those letters were very convincing, but even more convincing were the women who said that when they first started wearing suits, they didn't think it would help. They were only giving them a try or following a company dress code. After a short time 90 percent of them conceded that wearing suits worked—which means wearing suits works even for women who don't believe in them.

The new expanded suit wardrobe includes five types of suits. The first is the traditional "dress for success" suit. It imitates the colors and basic design of a man's suit. There are two versions of this suit: one with a jacket that looks very much like a man's jacket and a second cut the same style but without lapels. Both are high-authority suits, although the first works best with men while the second works equally well with both sexes. Suits with navy and medium gray jackets without lapels are ideal for interviews or the first day on a new job when you do not know with whom you will be dealing.

The second category is the "aggressive feminine" suit. A feminine suit becomes aggressive for one of two reasons: strong colors or strong patterns. Purple, red, and raspberry are illustrations of vibrant colors in these suits, while loud plaids, broad checks, and large herringbones are typical patterns. A good example of this type of suit is one Hillary Clinton wore the day her husband was inaugurated president of the United

States. The suit, which had a large-checked pattern, certainly was feminine, but it sent a strong message. It identified her as feminine and very powerful.

The third suit category is the "stylish professional" model. The jackets of most of these suits are designed to be worn without a blouse. They can come in a variety of colors and styles so they can send different messages. Most of them send a softer, more feminine message than the traditional imitation male dress for success suit, but they are always strong enough for the wearer to be taken seriously.

The fourth category is the "soft feminine" suit. The design or color can make a suit soft and feminine. Almost all suits in pastel colors fall into this category, as do many suits with feminine detailing, such as small felt collars or lace at the neck or sleeves.

Women who wear soft feminine suits generally choose pastel-colored models in warm climates. These suits *can* be effective. The best example is a very soft rich yellow suit; another, again from Hillary Clinton, is the pale green suit she wore when she first testified before Congress on health care. Both tested well.

However, most of the suits with feminine detailing are too "cute" to be effective. The only examples of feminine detailing I have seen that worked were on dark serious models with just one feminine detail. The best example was a black suit that would have been somber had it not been for lace detailing on the collar.

Unless a woman has a great deal of natural authority, she may have difficulty getting people, particularly men, to listen to her if she wears one of these ultrafeminine suits. However, if she works with the same people all the time and they recognize her as a professional, she can carry off this look, if the climate is appropriate.

The fifth category is the favorite suit of most powerful women: the conservative feminine suit. It has a conservative cut and color, but the color is one that would be found only in a woman's suit—for example, mahogany, dark plum, deep maroon, and the like. These suits send the message that most women want to send: that they are feminine and powerful. If they are rich looking, and most of them are, they work with the most powerful men and women.

If you are going to an important meeting, including an interview, and you do not know whether you are going to be dealing with a man or woman, wear a conservative feminine suit. It sends a positive message to most people.

Every woman should have one or two of these suits in her business wardrobe. If you own only one suit, it should be medium gray, but if you have two, the second should be a conservative feminine suit.

Naturally all suits that women wear do not fit neatly into one of these five categories. If you are not sure into which category to put a suit, and how and when to wear it, always place it in the least effective category. That way you will not make a mistake.

These divisions are important because men and women react differently to women wearing suits in each category. The men we surveyed and talked to in focus groups were most impressed by women wearing traditional "dress for success" suits. Our research showed that male executives, particularly men over fifty, were more likely to think a woman wearing a traditional blue, gray, or beige suit was competent and could be trusted. Most men over fifty-five actually gave greater credibility to a woman who had lapels on a suit.

The primary reason to wear a traditional suit—with or without lapels—is to add to your authority and professional-

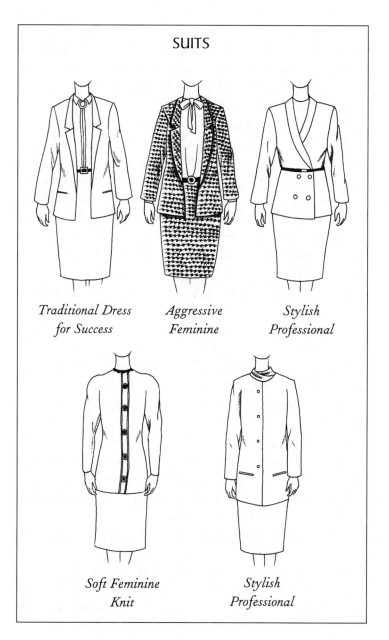

SUITS

Traditional Dress
for Success

Aggressive
Feminine

Stylish
Professional

Soft Feminine
Knit

Stylish
Professional

ism. These are the best suits to wear for job interviews and when you first deal with strangers. I recommend them for women working in male-dominated professions. I also strongly recommend them for women who find it difficult to be treated like equals by their male bosses and co-workers.

Dress for success suits also work in very conservative industries and when working in Asia. If you have a feeling you are not taken seriously, these suits will work for you.

Interestingly, the aggressive feminine suits didn't work particularly well with men or women. The only reason I included them is that so many businesswomen wear them. The women we surveyed said they love them and intend to continue to wear them. Twenty-six percent of these women said that they felt most confident when they were wearing one of these suits. In their minds these suits say "aggressive and feminine," and that is the message they want to send.

I recommend them for only three groups of women. They work best on—in fact, they have almost become a uniform for—women running for office. They also work on small women and very thin women of moderate height. The last group is women who work in overwhelmingly female-dominated companies.

Choosing one of these suits, however, can be tricky. If you choose the wrong color or wrong shade, the suit can appear lower class or even gaudy. The difference between an aggressive feminine suit and a horse blanket is sometimes just the shade of color or the angle of a design.

Never buy an aggressive feminine suit unless you are willing to pay top dollar. While women wearing these suits see themselves as effective, men sometimes see them as too aggressive.

A good example is the red suit. Most of the women I interviewed who own red suits thought of them as power garments.

I think they have been convinced by the fashion writers that red garments are by their nature powerful. Often they describe a woman in a red dress as powerful, and women believe them because when they have worn a red dress they felt a sense of power. Most do not realize that the reason they felt powerful when wearing a red suit is that red is a powerfully sexual color, which gives a woman the power to attract and manipulate men. However, unless you intend to use your sex appeal as a weapon in the office, a red suit is not effective, and a red dress is often a flag of failure.

If you have been having positive experiences in a red dress or in a red suit, it is because someone convinced you that it was powerful, and the fact that you felt powerful enables you to act powerfully.

The third suit category, the stylish professional, is the most useful addition to the original dress for success suits. Because they can be dark—navy and charcoal gray—and traditional, therefore, they can be very effective when dealing with conservative men.

Since they often come in midrange shades and light shades of traditional male colors—blue, gray, and beige—as well as serious feminine colors—maroon and forest green—both men and women treat women wearing them like professionals. And because they are cut in a conservative feminine style, carefully chosen accessories can change the wearer's look from serious to high fashion. All of these options make them the most useful suit for a woman who has to deal with a cross section of the business community.

The most effective examples of the final suit category, the soft feminine, are a rich pale yellow and a creamy beige. If you wish to wear one of these soft pastels, the suit must scream money. In a soft feminine suit most women see you as a competent professional; most men, however, will not. If you are dealing with men, wearing one of those suits is not a good idea; it will put you at a marked disadvantage. The only time the soft feminine suit is effective with men is when selling in the summer or in the South. Those colors are appropriate only when it is warm, and effective only when you are trying to coax someone into doing something. They are never effective when a woman is giving orders unless the woman is physically very large or has a very assertive personality.

The calendar research on soft summer suits shows that women were much more likely to have their authority and their competence challenged when wearing them than when wearing any other suit. If you have an authority problem, or you are petite, these suits are not for you.

Dyeing fabric in bright or subtle shades is very difficult. To achieve a rich look, the manufacturer has to use high-quality dyes and expensive material. Naturally the costs are passed on to the consumer. So if you want to wear light or bright colors, you are going to have to spend more money on your clothing than you do if you wear traditional conservative colors.

Limit your selection of suit colors to dark blue, medium-range blue, dark gray, medium gray, light gray, beige with a touch of gray, dark brown, medium brown, brown with gray, dark burgundy, tan, khaki, and forest green—and you can dress for less.

However, if you choose subtle pastels, pinks, pale blue, yellows, or very strong colors, such as red, lavender, or raspberry, you have to pay more and be very selective. This is also true if you choose suits with strong patterns. In order for the patterns to be crisp, neat, and rich looking, the manufacturer has to spend more and therefore pass along the cost. So if you have a limited budget, you have to limit your colors. Once you reach

that point in your career where you can afford to buy expensi
suits, you can choose subtle and vibrant colors.

Another reason for avoiding soft pastels and brightly color
garments is that they have limited usage. If you wear a navy s
once every two weeks, no one will remember when you wor
last. However, if you wear a bright red suit every other we
after a month of two your co-workers will think it is one of y
favorite suits. In order to wear suits that are vibrant or very
pastels, you have to have an extensive wardrobe.

Finally, conservative feminine suits that are traditional in
and are in conservative colors send positive messages to aln
everyone, and should be the backbone of most busin
women's suit wardrobes. If you have to deal with womer
men under 47 you should gradually replace half of your
and blue suits with these more feminine models.

HOW TO BUY A SUIT

Many women, particularly those who work in large cities, t
of shopping at their lunch hour as entertainment. They
through the stores and if an item strikes their fancy, they
it. That is not the way to buy a suit, because even if you
only one and seldom wear it, the suit may turn out to b
most important garment in your business wardrobe. Ever
isn't, suits by their nature are expensive and their sele
requires time and care.

The suit has been raised by men to a special position
right suit says that the wearer is educated, successful, pi
sional, powerful, and competent. A high-quality suit worr
appropriate accessories goes even further and identifie
wearer as a member of business's ruling class. Therefore

chasing the suit is an important undertaking and should not be engaged in haphazardly.

Before you go to buy a suit, take inventory of your wardrobe. Decide whether or not you need a suit. Once you decide that you need one, you should start thinking about what type of suit will best fit your situation. Are you buying the suit for a particular meeting or to balance your wardrobe? If you are going for a job interview, you probably need a serious suit, but if you already own too many high-authority suits, you may decide to buy one that sends a friendlier message.

After watching women buy suits for almost twenty years, I have found that they make better selections if, before they go shopping, they decide exactly which suit they want. Women have told us they made wiser purchases when they chose the color, pattern, weight, material, and style before they entered the store. Even when they were not able to find exactly what they wanted and had to settle, making these decisions ahead of time stopped them from buying on impulse.

Because the suit is the essential part of your wardrobe, when you go to buy a suit, wear the most expensive and best suit you have. If you do not own a suit, wear the best conservative outfit you own.

There are three reasons for doing this. First, in most women's clothing departments being well dressed makes it easier to attract sales clerks. Second, most large stores have a number of tailors working on suits. Their skills may range from the Leonardo da Vinci of tailoring to a novice who keeps sticking himself with a needle. In many stores the fitters pay careful attention to the person they are fitting and indicate on the fitting form what type of person she is. If the customer looks as if she is going to be demanding, they indicate it on the form, and that determines the level of tailoring she receives. A clerk

in one store told me everyone who purchased a suit was graded from A to F. Those who received A's were blessed because the Leonardo da Vinci of tailoring altered their suits with skill and care. Those who were graded F did not fare well at all; the fellow who regularly stuck himself with the needle was given their suits to alter. The customer's rating was made by clerks, most of whom come from limited backgrounds. The only thing they had in common is they were impressed with customers who were well dressed. Third, a majority of the businesswomen we interviewed said that when they dressed stylishly sales clerks catered to them, but when they were not well dressed the same clerks ignored them or treated them poorly. So when you deal with clerks, dress to kill.

Once you decide that the store does not have the suit you need, leave immediately. Our researchers accompanied women buying suits, but they did not interfere with their purchasing decisions. They only watched and questioned them after they made a purchase. The researchers reported that often when women didn't find what they wanted, they settled for something less, sometimes quite a bit less.

I understand that for many of you shopping is a chore. If you are like many of my clients, managing your time is a top priority. You are goal oriented, not recreational shoppers. Nevertheless, you should never settle when you are buying a suit. A suit should be looked upon as an investment in your future.

If you find a suit that meets your requirements, the first thing you must do is grab hold of the sleeve and squeeze it for at least ten seconds. When you let go, if the wrinkles don't fall out immediately, reject that suit. If the suit passes the grab test, look at the material and ask yourself three questions.

First, does this material look rich and expensive? If the answer is no, keep looking.

Second, would a successful, elegant, stylish woman in my industry wear this suit? No? Pass.

Third, is it a suitable color and style for a woman in my industry, company, and position? Will the decision makers in my company be impressed with the suit?

Take the next step only if your answers to these three questions are yes.

Your next step should be to read the label and find out what the suit is made of. If the material is acceptable, pick up the collar and look at the stitching. It should be neat and reinforced. Examine the lining. See that it is attached securely. All jackets, unless they are summer jackets, should be lined. Also check the exterior and interior pockets. See if the interior pockets are really functional. In some women's suits they put pockets inside that are such a peculiar size, you can't use them. You want pockets that you can use.

Next, examine the buttonholes. They must look as if they are going to stand up to constant wear. Good buttonholes are the hallmarks of a well-made suit. After that, look at the buttons. The quality of the button is often a good indicator of the quality of the suit. Cheap plastic buttons are usually found on inexpensive suits, while expensive bone or fancy buttons are often found on expensive suits. You will also want to note whether they have been attached securely. Are extra buttons attached inside the jacket?

Finally, take the suit back to the dressing room. Before you put on the skirt, examine it independently. Make sure the seams are neatly sewn, the zipper is covered, and that it has been attached with care. Has the waist been reinforced? If not, do not even try it on. Look for detailing in the pockets and pay particular attention to how neatly they lie. Then look at the rest of the jacket. Pay careful attention to where the sleeve has been attached and to the way the seam has been finished. These are good indicators of how well the jacket is made and how well the suit will stand up to wear.

Women make one major mistake when it comes to fitting suits. Most of the clothing women buy—dresses, blouses, and so on—is unstructured. If a dress or another unstructured garment does not fit properly when they first try it on, they do not reject it out of hand. They know a good tailor can usually fix it.

This is not true of suits. When you put on a suit jacket, unless it hangs comfortably on you, do not even think about purchasing it. Unless the shoulders fit perfectly, you are wasting your money. The shoulders of a coat are very much like the frame of a building. Most construction people will put a new facing on it, gut it, and redesign the inside, but they do not want to work on the frame. Experience has taught them that doing so is very tricky and usually not worthwhile. Good alteration departments do not want to play with the shoulders for the same reason—it is too tricky and not worthwhile. If the shoulders in a suit don't fit when you first put it on, do not buy it. If you love a garment and the store says it can be fixed and you are determined to get it fixed, do not put down a large deposit. Sometimes they succeed and sometimes they do not.

HOW TO CHOOSE THE BEST MATERIALS FOR SUITS

The best material for a suit is wool. Wool usually takes to dyes better than any other fabric; it doesn't lose its shape, it is resilient, it lies on the body very neatly, in winter it is warmer, and if you get a tropical-weight suit in the summer, it can be quite cool. In addition, wool can be woven in a variety of different patterns. Most important, wool or the look of wool says upper middle class, executive, and elite. It is the nonverbal message that the richness of wool sends that is most important.

The second-best fabric for a suit is a blend, usually a manmade fiber combined with wool. The rule of thumb is, if the blend is less than 50 percent wool, it will not look as rich as wool. There are exceptions to this rule, but not many. When you buy a blend, you want the look of wool, and unless the material looks as rich and as luxurious as wool, it sends the wrong message. If you are not sure what message a suit sends, do not even consider buying it. Even subtle differences in the look and feel of suiting material can change a suit from a power garment to a peasant garment.

Unless you can afford a good wool suit, a blend may be a better choice. Cheap all-wool suits may look good on the rack and even pass the grab test because the sizing gives the material a certain resilience when new, but after being dry-cleaned a half dozen times they can look like a damp rag. There are always exceptions, but all-wool suits that cost less than $250 usually turn out to be a poor investment.

Some suits, of course, are made of 100 percent man-made materials. There is only one way of judging suits made of this material: how well it imitates a rich wool suit. People who make fabrics have come up with wonderful materials that look just like wool. Some are almost as rich looking as decent wool and they can be tailored to lie neatly on the body, so if you choose very carefully, they can work. In addition, they have the built-in advantage that they almost never wrinkle. People who travel for a living, particularly those who spend much of their day behind the wheel, love man-made fibers. However, since most blends are wrinkle resistant and almost invariably look richer than man-made fibers, I recommend blends.

A number of women, particularly those in the Sun Belt, favor cotton and linen suits. There is no question that they are extremely comfortable. However, unless the material has been treated to make it wrinkle resistant, in just a couple of hours you will look as if you have been wearing it all day.

Pure cotton wrinkles, quickly and easily. Some men can get away with the rumpled look; women cannot. If a woman looks rumpled or disheveled, most people think she is not sophisticated or competent. It is not a look you can afford, and it certainly is not a look you should pay for.

The rule for suits is that they must be made of wool or look as if they were. Ninety-five percent of knit suits do not test well, nor do suits made of corduroy, denim, or any other materials associated with leisure wear.

Exception to the rule: A silk suit can work. I met an engineer in Denver wearing a conservative navy silk suit. She told me she saved that suit for her most important meetings. She bragged that the presidents of Fortune 500 companies and half the women she met complimented her on her suit. It looked very rich and businesslike. I was so impressed, I took a picture of the suit and tested it. When we showed pictures of her in that suit to a cross section of businesspeople, 97 percent thought she was a competent and very successful executive. It tested as well as any suit we ever tested.

When I received the results, I called and asked her where she had purchased the suit. She said that two years before she had consulted with a California bank. While she was there several women at the bank spent one lunch hour having suits made by a Hong Kong tailor, and they invited her to join them. She ordered the navy suit and wished she had ordered several more.

About four months later she recommended me, and I was hired by that bank. As soon as I arrived I saw that half the women were wearing similar silk suits. The women were crazy about them. They thought that at $300 apiece they were a great bargain. The first time the tailor showed up he had only three colors: navy, medium-range gray, and a dark brown with a green tint. These original suits all tested well. When he returned the next year he brought a number of additional swatches to choose from. The new swatches were pale yellow, pale pink, pale green, forest green, and a cream-colored beige. In addition, he brought blue herringbone and a gray pinstripe. About twenty women at the bank bought at least one or two suits from him the second time he came. The minute I saw the suits I knew there was something wrong. My gut instinct said they didn't work. When I tested them, I saw I was right. The women in the pinstripe suits looked like clowns while the women in the pale pastel suits looked as though they were attending a garden party rather than working for a major bank. This is a typical example of suiting material that works only in a very limited range of colors and patterns. That is why choosing fabrics other than wool can be very tricky.

A few weeks after I finished this research I was in New York and ran across a successful woman wearing another navy silk suit. She had bought it in Italy and paid several times what the women in Denver paid.

She was kind enough to let me test it. It tested fairly well, but it wasn't nearly as effective as the original navy silk suit. The suits were almost identical, but not quite. While the engineer's blue suit, on a scale of one to ten, was a ten, the blue suit worn by the executive in New York, which cost three times as much, was a four. Its main drawback was that it sent the message to most of the men she met that the wearer was not a serious businessperson. In fact, it looked too rich and dressy to work in business. After I reported back to the woman as I had promised, she told me she already had come to the same conclusion.

When you have suits made of any material other than wool or one that looks like wool, you are taking a chance.

CREDIBILITY OUTFITS

Women naturally have a higher credibility than men. Our sales research showed that men and women are much more likely to believe a woman than a man when both make questionable statements. A man's credibility is constantly being questioned. This rarely happens to a woman, which gives her a tremendous advantage when selling new, untried ideas or products and is a tremendous asset when managing people. One of the signs of effective leaders is that they are trusted.

However, not all women are credible, and there are a number of outfits that can help if you have the problem of not being believed. A medium-range blue suit with a white blouse is the highest credibility outfit a woman can wear. A navy blue suit with a white blouse is second. Third is a beige suit with a touch of gray in it, with a light blue blouse. Fourth, a tan suit with a medium-range blue blouse. Fifth, the camel suit with a medium-range blue blouse. Sixth, a pale yellow suit with either a beige or light blue blouse.

Although all these suits tested well, the first two—medium blue and navy—were by far the best. The key to being credible is not creating any visual surprises. You do not want to wear the latest fashion or a look that no one has seen. You should wear things that people have seen over and over again. Do not worry about looking good. Women who are tastefully put together have no more credibility than women who seem to lack a sense of style. The critical factor in credibility is presenting an expected image. You have to look the way most people expect you to look. If you are a banker, you must look like a banker; if you are a scientist, you must look like a scientist; and if you are an artist, you must look like an artist. Don't wear anything that will surprise the people you meet.

POPULARITY

Today I spend half my time teaching classes on popularity. When I discovered that the key characteristic of a salesperson's success is her popularity, I started to research the subject. For my book on popularity, my first research was aimed at discovering if the way you dressed could affect your popularity. We found that certain colors and color combinations did make the wearer seem more friendly and, therefore, more popular. Light blue, pale yellow, beige, camel, and tan, along with most earth tones, made the wearer seem friendlier and more approachable. The combination of navy with pale yellow or beige also sent a friendly message.

We further discovered that when a woman is dealing with men, in most corporate environments she seems more friendly wearing a suit without a lapel. The look is softer and more feminine, and most men respond positively to it.

However, a woman has to walk a very narrow line. If she sends signals that are so feminine that they are read as sexual, it has the opposite effect. This surprises most women, but sexual signals in an office setting, while seeming to please most men, do not. Most men are either annoyed or intimidated by women in the office who dress for sex.

Women who believe that a tough and aggressive style will help them to succeed are mistaken. There are exceptions to the rule, but most women with power are charmers, and even those who present a rough exterior to subordinates charm the people above them. Over the last eight years the style that has tested best has gone from openly aggressive and somewhat masculine to quietly assertive and feminine.

In addition, we found that most popular women used clothing in the same way. First, they dressed like members of a team. They didn't dress in a way that separated them visually from their co-workers. If everyone in their office was stylish, they were stylish. If the rest of the company dressed conservatively, they were conservative. Second, while remaining within the range of the unofficial/official dress code of the office, they were often one of the better dressers.

Third, their style was usually feminine. Although they could wear high-powered clothing, they were much more likely to wear suits without lapels when they did. Fourth, they had a certain informality about them. They generally looked as if they were well put together but didn't care that much about it. Their hairstyles were short, they sometimes walked with their jackets opened, and they seemed relaxed about their appearance.

Finally, they never dressed in a manner that was overtly sexual. This turned off everyone in every office except, of course, the person they were trying to seduce.

HIGH-AUTHORITY SUITS

The darker and obviously more expensive a garment, the more authority it gives its wearer. That is why most executives in large companies and Hell's Angels wear dark uniforms. If you want to add to your authority, charcoal gray, black, and navy suits are the answer.

Mary, like most of the women managers in her very conservative company, wore suits regularly. When I looked at her wardrobe I told her to buy two high-authority suits because she complained she sometimes had trouble getting male executives to listen to her ideas. Their reaction was not a surprise; her wardrobe was terminally cute. Every outfit said soft, young, and feminine. Mary made the mistake that many women make. They think they look good in one type of outfit, so they buy an entire wardrobe of similar outfits.

Mary was married to an attorney who bought her my video consultation as a birthday gift. When he saw she ignored my advice he followed up by buying her two serious suits for Christmas, a navy solid and a pinstripe charcoal gray. Once Mary started wearing them her world changed. Management started listening to her ideas, and in two years she received two promotions and her salary almost doubled.

The real trick when choosing any garment, including suits, is to ask yourself whom you are going to be dealing with and what message you want to send them. Then pick an outfit that will help you send that message.

Chapter Three

The Dress

Women have worn dresses since the beginning of recorded history. As different as the traditional Japanese kimono, the Indian sari, the gowns of medieval Europe, and the modern shirtwaist are, they are all dresses. Before *The Woman's Dress for Success Book* was published in 1977, the dress was the dominant garment in most women's social and business wardrobes. Therefore it is not surprising that when we asked men in the early 1970s to close their eyes and describe a working woman, over 95 percent described a woman in a dress.

Prior to 1977 women wore suits and jackets to work, but they were the exception, not the rule. When Rosalind Russell played the "misguided" hard-driven businesswoman in the forties who in the end would give up her career, marry the man, and live happily ever after, she wore suits. When she "came to her senses" and surrendered to a man, she wore dresses.

At the time, even sophisticated men and women believed there was something perverse about a woman wearing the male symbol of power, the suit. In fact, in the 1940s propaganda films Hollywood often portrayed female Nazi spies as masculine women wearing men's suits with shirts and ties. Real women, decent women, feminine women, and loyal American women wore more feminine outfits. They wore dresses because the vast majority of both men and women, prior to the last third of the twentieth century in the United States, believed that women were made by God and nature to be submissive to men, and a feminine dress is a garment of submission.

One of the first steps I took when researching women's clothing was to hire a fashion designer to identify the basic designs in dresses and other garments. She came up with 646 different dresses, ranging from extremely conservative models to those with very short skirts and plunging necklines. Using pictures of these dresses, we surveyed a cross section of the American business community.

In the early 1970s we questioned mainly male executives because they were the people with power. There were a few women in executive positions at that time, but most had no real power. They were women who had either fought their way into the male-dominated executive suites through sheer force of will, intellect, and ability or been placed in executive positions as window dressing. Many companies had one or two token women in their executive ranks. They were usually in charge of public relations, a field in which women were successful before the women's movement. Possibly they'd been promoted through a women's program, which usually meant that a position had been created for them. Their real function was to see to it that groups fighting for equal opportunities for women were kept at a distance. Surveying these women would have been meaningless during that period, so I mainly tested the reactions of men to women's clothing. I did survey the few women I knew who had fought their way into the male-dominated executive and professional ranks, but I had to search for them.

The first step was to test dresses as a category. Our only meaningful finding was that very conservative dresses in dark colors announced that the wearer might be a competent businesswoman, while dresses in lighter colors or with feminine patterns said she was not. Please note I said they announced that the wearer *might* be a competent businesswoman, not that she *was* one. At the time, dresses were worn by all women, so they did not identify the wearer as a businesswoman. That was why although I said businesswomen could wear dark conservative dresses to work, I did not recommend they do so.

In the early seventies, when we tested dresses against other garments, what surprised me was not that the skirted suit won, or that women wearing jackets tested better than women without jackets, or that conservative dresses tested better than frilly ones—it was that dresses tested so poorly. It also surprised me to find out that if a woman dressed in an outfit that sent a sexual message, both men and women didn't take her seriously. In fact, the women gave women wearing sexy garments lower ratings than the men did. The reason I was so surprised is that all my life I have been surrounded by effective women. My grandmother, who thought I was the center of the universe, started her own business and was very successful. My mother worked most of her life as a statistician. She taught me to cook because at least twice a week the telephone rang the minute she walked in the house. I had to cook dinner because Mother was too busy explaining to her male bosses how to solve problems they were struggling with. My wife worked as a nurse and supported us both so I could start this business.

Naturally, since I was surrounded by competent capable businesswomen, I thought of women as being as effective as men and was shocked to learn that the vast majority of men and women did not agree with me. Even today, if a woman wears a feminine, sexy, or frilly dress, 58 percent of the men and 33 percent of the women who meet her for the first time think that she is not a serious or effective businessperson.

The accomplishments and progress of American working women in the last twenty years has affected the way most businessmen perceive women and the way women perceive themselves. Seventy-two percent of businesspeople today think that a woman in a dress can be effective. The problem is, 28 percent do not, and 93 percent of those think that she would be more effective if she wore a jacket with the dress. This is very important, because not every woman who appears effective gets hired, promoted, or put in charge of important projects. In most cases, jobs, promotions, and other rewards of success are given to the woman who appears more effective than her competition.

The greatest change in the last twenty years has been men's attitude toward a feminine woman's ability to be effective in business. In the early 1970s only 16 percent of men thought a woman wearing a traditional feminine dress might be an effective businessperson, while today close to 70 percent of men assume that a woman wearing a dress might be effective.

There are two problems with wearing dresses to work, even in the 1990s. First, 26 percent of women and 31 percent of men do not think of the average woman in a dress as authoritative or effective. In their opinion nothing significant has changed in the last twenty years, and our interviews indicate that they are not about to change their minds. Second, even the men and women who perceive a woman in a feminine dress as effective find it difficult to think of her as a competitive executive or professional.

Strangely, the success of the jacket and the feminine suit, along with the success of women in convincing themselves and men that they are competent, has hurt the dress as a business garment. When I first looked at how people responded to businesswomen in different outfits, only women in conservative suits were seen by most as effective. Women wearing anything else were seen by the majority of well-educated and successful men and women as ineffective and unprofessional. Most people twenty years ago thought the dress was no less effective or less appropriate than feminine suits or jacket outfits. Nevertheless many women who wore dresses were promoted. The same managers who believed that a woman in a dress was probably not effective felt no hesitation promoting a woman who wore dresses once she proved she was effective.

A number of the same executives in the 1970s said they would not move a man into management who did not wear a suit because he did not dress like a manager. There was a uniform for men, and everyone knew it. Any man who refused to wear the uniform was thought of as a rebel or a fool and not management material. In most companies this eliminated him from serious consideration for a management slot.

Today, because the jacket outfit is an almost universally recognized uniform for businesswomen, any woman who does not wear one is eliminated from serious consideration for a management job for the same reasons a man who does not wear a suit is eliminated. In addition, since most women compete with other women for management or executive slots and 62 percent of them wear suits or jacket outfits, a woman who wears dresses puts herself at a real disadvantage.

I know that the fashion writers regularly tell women that they can and should wear the latest dresses to work. They usually argue that a particular dress is stylish and if you wear one you are making a statement—or that clever, successful women wear whatever they want and are often trendsetters. In the future the clever ones will probably quote my research to show that women have forced men to accept colorful, stylish feminine suits and jacket outfits. Their argument will be that it is your duty as a strong, independent woman to stand up to male prejudice and stupidity. What they will not point out is that the women who make the fashion breakthroughs wearing stylish dresses or other trendy looks are not the women who get the promotions and higher salaries.

For four years we followed the careers of 161 women with advanced degrees. Most of them were working for client companies, and neither they nor their bosses knew their progress was being audited independently. At the inception of the study we asked their co-workers to place them into one of three groups of dressers: conservative, average, and fashionable. The definition changed from industry to industry, company to company, office to office, and, of course, one section of the country to another. Even though only 17 percent of these women were considered fashionable dressers by their co-workers, we kept looking until we found three equal groups of sixty. At the end of four years we had three groups of forty-seven. While many of the women changed the way they dressed over time, most did not.

We used income as a way of measuring success because numbers do not lie. With this measurement the conservative group was by far the most successful. In spite of this, half were no longer dressing conservatively at the end of the study. In spite of their success they were convinced by the fashion press directly or through their peers that women no longer had to dress conservatively to succeed. The average dressers, after six years, were earning only slightly more money than their fashionable sisters. However, the raw statistics are misleading. Seven from the fashionable groups became very successful, and their salaries offset the more evenly spread rise among the average dressers. In addition, five of the seven were in high-fashion industries. Included in this group are three superstars, a TV personality, a media lawyer, and a woman who sells luxury items to the very rich. The combined salaries of these three were almost one-fourth the total earned by the other forty-four women in the group. A high-fashion look undoubtedly is a tremendous asset in some high-fashion jobs, while it is a liability in more traditional jobs.

If you are one of the first in your office or your industry to wear something fashionable or daring, a look that in five years all the other women in your office will be able to wear without hurting their careers, you may be jeopardizing your career. Until executives, particularly male executives, are conditioned by seeing a number of effective women in that look, they will treat women wearing it poorly.

Unfortunately most women who are leaders in fashion are followers in middle American industry. When I showed the research to three focus groups made up of female executives and managers, the vast majority agreed that it was terrible and unfair—but true. And only one of twenty-six executives said she would be willing to risk her career for the freedom of wearing what she wanted. One woman seemed to speak for the others when she said, "I work in the real world, not an ideal world. Daily, I deal with men who are as chauvinistic as any in the Dark Ages. I discovered, the hard way, that it is more difficult to get their respect and cooperation when I wear feminine or fashionable outfits. So I don't wear them to work."

In spite of the research at least a million fairly successful women today wear dresses most of the time. The reason that they can wear dresses and succeed is that the message sent by a businesswoman in a dress has changed, because the position of women in society has changed. As I pointed out earlier, a woman wearing a dress, unless it is too cute, too feminine, or too sexy for business, is no longer looked upon automatically as a lightweight. Another reason some women can get away with wearing dresses is that businesspeople, whose initial reaction was negative, today usually change their minds if the woman has a title such as vice president, managing engineer, or something similar.

In addition, the dress of women who interact with the same people every day has little impact on their co-workers' opinion of them. If the other people know that they are hardworking and talented, they will be respected. They will not be judged on the way they dress because a better way of judging is available. However, if a woman has not made a strong positive or negative impression or has to deal with strangers, she will be judged, at least partially, on what she is wearing. If she is wearing a dress, particularly a light colored or femininely styled model, those strangers are less likely to trust her professional judgment or ability to lead.

There are, of course, exceptions to every rule. Dresses work far better than suits or jacket outfits for the small percentage of women who are very aggressive or whose size, style, or personality makes them intimidating. Years ago I advised Denise, a bank manager who was over six feet tall, to wear dresses whenever she could. She refused because she worked in a very conservative bank. I admitted that I was guessing and she might be right, but I challenged her to keep an image calendar and test my theory. After six months she wrote to admit I had been right, adding that she was now wearing dresses most of the time. As I had advised, she continued to wear her suits to meetings at corporate headquarters. When she moved to headquarters I told her to continue to wear dresses, but she refused. She had become one of the top executives in the bank and claimed no woman in power could wear a dress.

When Janet Reno, to whom Denise bears a resemblance, became U.S. attorney general, Denise once again started wearing dresses and reported she had less difficulty getting the men in the office to cooperate with her. Dresses soften a woman's image and make her less threatening. For some women this can be a critical factor.

Dresses can also be used to solve particular problems. Susan, a very successful saleswoman who works for a large computer company, found that the new purchasing agent for her best client reacted angrily when she tried to be her usual assertive self. He made her wait two hours to see him on her second visit. Her instincts told her to soften her approach, so the next time she wore a feminine dress. Like all good salespeople, she changed her approach when she found out what she was doing was not working. She said once she put on a dress he became very friendly.

When I presented this problem to my phone tag group they agreed that women run across men who are easily intimidated and cannot stand women with power. They were divided almost in half on how to handle these men: turn feminine or turn ferocious. While they did not agree on which tactic was most effective, a majority admitted they would employ whichever method they thought would work best. In one focus group, when a vice president of a bank said she often used feminine charm to disarm male chauvinists, she was immediately challenged by a younger member of the group. The second woman argued that using feminine wiles was an admission that these men had the right to be jackasses just because they were men. She said when she ran across such jerks she went straight for the jugular.

The vice president said that ten years earlier she'd thought the same way, but since then she had learned two things: all the real killers are charmers, and in business the only fight you win is the one you avoid. She added that her motto is "Make progress, not enemies."

In three different sessions with my telephone tag team, all members agreed that if a woman is in a business where women in power wear conservative dresses, she should do so as well. However, they also agreed that even at the times a woman decides that wearing a dress is the way to go, she should keep a jacket close at hand.

I go from company to company, lecturing on corporate dress, and in most companies my lectures follow a format. I usually give a two-hour lecture to both men and women, followed by individual consultations. If we are setting up a corporate dress code, I run focus groups with a cross section of the people in the company and the executives before lecturing or before doing individual consultations. In spite of mountains of research I have on women in dresses and the overwhelming evidence that a woman in anything but the most conservative tailored dress is not as effective as a woman in a jacket or suit, I can predict, in one in four engagements, the great dress debate will take place. Most businesswomen in the Sun Belt and in the summer wear dresses to work. They are married to the comfort of the dress and have convinced themselves that they are as effective wearing a dress as they are in anything else.

When the research will not convince women that dresses make them less effective I have them keep a Dress for Success calendar, in which they record the reactions of their subordinates, superiors, and co-workers to them wearing various outfits, including dresses. The calendars kept by these women, who frequently were out to prove that dresses worked, often surprised them. Most found that when they had to talk their male boss into doing anything, they had more luck when they wore jackets over their dresses. They also agreed that when enlisting the cooperation of relative strangers—say, people in other departments—they didn't do as well in dresses as in suits or jacket outfits. Even the women who wore dresses all the time concluded dresses didn't work as well as suits or jacket outfits when asking other people to make major commitments.

Another thing the calendar research showed us was that the socioeconomic message sent by a dress was more important than the one sent by a suit or jacket outfit. If an executive, manager, or professional wears a dress, it must look rich. In some companies I conduct individual consultations only after the employee has kept a Dress for Success (or DFS) calendar for at least six months. When the calendar showed that a particular dress worked well with both men and women, it invariably screamed money. Unfortunately, the best way to guarantee that a dress screams money is to spend a great deal of money buying it. Dresses bought in the most expensive stores tested better than dresses bought in moderately priced stores, and the dresses bought in moderately priced stores tested better than dresses bought in discount stores.

However, if you know what you are doing, you can buy a moderately priced executive dress. Individual tastes weigh so heavily here that it is difficult to set rules. When we surveyed the women whose dress wardrobes were most effective, we found that the majority of them were raised at their daddy's pin-striped knee. Interestingly, even when their mothers worked, their fathers taught them the rules for dressing in corporate America.

* * *

The one group of women for whom dresses work are executive wives. That is because the dress sends the message that you are an old-fashioned wife and your primary role is to support your husband. Companies will deny that this is the type of person they want their executives to marry, but most of them will be lying to themselves, if to no one else. When you attend an affair at your husband's company, you want to appear to be a supportive wife and not an independent career woman. Companies are less likely to promote a man if they think his wife has a career as important as his. This is the time and the place to wear a dress.

Since I know that some women will insist on wearing dresses to work, I researched which dresses worked best. The models that tested best were expensive, conservative, and purchased in upscale stores. While the choice of acceptable colors, fabrics, and designs in suits and jackets has expanded dramatically in the past twenty years, the dresses that tested well in the 1970s still test well today.

The colors that work best are deep blue, navy, tan, beige, medium-range blue, grayish brown, and dark brown. I recommend dark gray, but light gray and rust, which I recommended in the seventies, are so much less effective than suits and jacket outfits that I no longer recommend them.

The dresses that send a positive message to male executives are in male colors and tailored. Their message is, "I'm in charge." Most tailored conservative dresses in darker shades of brown, maroon, and green send an executive message. The most important characteristic of dress colors is that they are upper middle class. The shades of color that worked best were subtle not strong, vibrant not electric, rich not cheap. If you were raised in an upper-middle-class environment, you can probably trust your conditioning when choosing dresses. However, if you come from a less privileged background, you must cross-shop.

The dress colors that tested poorly were all shades of green (except forest green), orange, light rust, bright yellow, lavender, pink, mustard, and red, especially European red, which sometimes has an orange tint. If you are a fashionable dresser, watch out for this, since it is a favorite of many European designers.

Black dresses fall into a special category. The reason many test poorly is that they are often too dressy for the office. A few tailored black dresses did test well, but I still advise women that unless they come from a sophisticated background and are sure they have a feel for clothing, they should avoid black dresses. Black dresses are usually too formal or too funereal to wear to work; it is a dress color women should save for night.

The material that tested best was wool. Heavy-looking wools, like tweed and herringbone, and gabardine were particularly effective. Generally, dresses for the fall season tested best. Executives wearing these dresses were seen as top-notch by almost everyone they met. Cotton and a number of blends also tested well. Natural fibers were twice as likely to send an upper-middle-class message as blends. The blends that contained cotton and wool and looked like cotton or wool tested best, but dozens of man-made materials, such as polypropylene, tested beautifully.

Dresses made of obvious man-made materials, especially polyester, tested poorly. While some textured polyesters worked, most polyester dresses tested so poorly that my researchers started calling them "peasant dresses." The dresses that worked were usually made of fibers that looked rich, starched, and substantial. If a man-made fiber sends this message, it can be just as acceptable as a natural fiber. The only fibers you must avoid in dresses are those that send a sexual message because they are either transparent or clingy.

Obviously we couldn't test every pattern found in dresses. The only pattern that made dresses more effective was the pinstripe found in men's suits. A conservative pinstripe tailored woman's dress is more authoritative than most suits, while at the same time less threatening and more fashionable. In medium to dark blue and gray it is almost an ideal outfit. We found only two instances when it does not work on a woman: if she is speaking or going for an interview, a pinstripe dress is a problem. I think the reason is that at certain distances pinstripes can be difficult to look at and could be distracting. Still, it is the only pattern that works better than a solid.

There are a few guidelines that can help you choose dress patterns. A dress with traditional feminine patterns such as florals say housewife, not businesswoman. Businesswomen wearing these reported that neither men nor women took them seriously. The only time feminine prints work is when they are small and on a dark, conservative dress. Usually the smaller the pattern, the more effective the dress. When we showed pictures of women wearing conservatively cut dresses with large patterns—particularly feminine ones, brightly colored geometric patterns, flowers, and so on—and asked men and women to guess the wearers' jobs, 84 percent of the men and 66 percent of the women guessed the wearers were either secretaries or clerks. When we showed the same people dresses with similar designs and colors but small neat patterns, 62 percent of the men and only 37 percent of the women identified the wearers as secretaries or clerks.

Dresses that are designed with accent colors—such as a navy blue dress with a white piping or a brown dress with an orange panel—are sometimes very effective. Dresses like this work best when the accent color makes up no more than 20 percent of the dress. Do not be turned off by a bright accent color.

DRESSES

Dress with matching jacket

Simple shirtwaist

Tailored dress

SUCCESS DRESS
PATTERNS FOR THE OFFICE

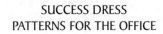

Solid

Plaid

Stripe

On the right dress it adds to the wearer's sense of presence by drawing attention to her without taking away from her business image. It's the overall impact that counts. The first consideration in buying a bicolored dress is the primary color. It must be conservative, traditional, and upper class. Secondary colors only have to be tasteful. If a dress has two strong colors, both must be upper class and traditional, while only one has to be conservative.

Trust your instincts. We showed a cross section of businesswomen pictures of 120 business dresses. The selection included models that were bright, dull, conservative, fashionable, sexy, and cute, and 90 percent of the women knew which dresses would work in their businesses. Their only problem was with language. We showed these same dresses to men and asked them to pick out the serious dresses. The dresses they called "serious" business dresses had been identified by the women as "very serious." If you work with men, in choosing a dress, you must ask, Does it send a "very" serious business message? If the answer is no, do not buy it.

We showed 126 businessmen the pictures just described and asked them to pick out the women they would be willing to take with them to make a presentation to their most important client. One hundred and two of them picked the same nineteen dresses. Seventeen of the nineteen were in traditional male colors. The other two were dark green and maroon. All nineteen were tailored.

When I asked an all-female focus group for their reaction to this research, two women said it was hard to believe. I then told them we surveyed men in their company and several came from their office. They asked me if they could talk to the men. I picked up the phone, and in less than ten minutes four men arrived. One was the executive vice president of the company, one was a manager in the marketing department, and two were engineers, one in his twenties and the other in his forties.

As soon as the men entered the room, one woman, pointing to the pictures, asked them if they really liked and trusted dull and boring. I think that she expected the men to apologize sheepishly. The vice president did not answer her but congratulated me on getting the point across that men thought that way. Then the older engineer added that he would not bring any woman with him unless she was wearing a suit. When the women pointed out that he was not wearing a suit, he said he would wear a suit. After the shouting died down, he backed off a bit. He said he would insist the women wear suits only if men attending were wearing suits. The exchange lasted for about fifteen minutes, and then the men left. One of the women stood up and announced they had just proven that men are idiots who make unreasonable demands on women and it was time they stopped putting up with their narrow-minded idiocy. The debate ended when a manager asked whether the woman speaking thought the fellows who had just left would be more likely to promote a woman who told them they were idiots or one who pretended they were not. When she did not answer, the manager said that she was going to continue to pretend.

In addition to testing which patterns, textures, and materials made a woman look most effective, we tested which dress colors, patterns, and materials attracted men. A number of women we surveyed asked us to find out if there were colors and patterns that performed well in both areas. The three colors that sent the message that the wearer was efficient and attractive were navy, beige, and medium-range blue. Although these colors worked with all groups, we did most of our testing with men who were college graduates.

While men see women dressed in gray as very effective,

they do not find women wearing gray to be attractive. In fact, gray dresses are a real turnoff. Possibly that is why they look upon women wearing gray as effective. When any woman dresses for work she has to decide what product she wants to sell and package herself accordingly. It is not fair—men can look very effective and sexy while women cannot—but in most cases it is true.

There is no question that dresses make women look sexy, attractive, and feminine—and those are the best reasons most women should not wear them to work.

Chapter Four

Completing Your Business Wardrobe

SKIRTS

In those old black-and-white movies that today you can see only at two o'clock in the morning on cable, Hollywood gangsters with Brooklyn accents refer to their women as "skirts." The women are invariably lower class and trashy. Being referred to as a skirt was not a compliment in the thirties. In the early seventies, when I researched *The Woman's Dress for Success Book*, nothing had changed. When I showed pictures of women wearing skirts to businesspeople of both sexes and asked them to describe the women in the pictures, most said they were lower class, unsophisticated, and at best high school graduates. Over 75 percent guessed that they worked as receptionists, clerks, or secretaries. Ninety-two percent did not think the women in the pictures had serious career plans. Women in skirts were almost never described as bright, well educated, sophisticated, successful, or powerful.

The first time I researched the skirt in 1967 I had my people show pictures of women in skirt outfits to a hundred executives at a convention in Chicago. I was so surprised by the responses that I instructed the researchers to redo the survey. The second time I had them tell the respondents that women in the pictures were executives, lawyers, managers, stockbrokers, etc., before asking for their opinions. Fifty-two percent of the women and 83 percent of the men didn't think these women were serious businesspeople in spite of their credentials. And without our asking, many went on to say the women probably weren't career minded or too good at what they did. In the 1970s the skirt was a flag of failure.

Today that is not true. A skirt can send a very positive message, but only when it looks as if it might be part of a suit. We received positive responses most often in offices where both men and women take off their jackets. The skirts that tested best were in male suiting colors or dark conservative feminine suiting colors and were very conservatively cut. While women today can wear colorful suits to the office and be considered effective, they will not be taken seriously if they wear colorful skirts without jackets or vests that look as if they might be part of a suit. Since 1989, when we showed pictures of women in skirts to men, over 90 percent of them identified women wearing light, frilly, short, or sexy skirts in much the same way that women in skirts were described in the 1930s. Even today, when businesspeople identified a woman wearing a skirt as a professional or an executive, 19 percent of the men directly or indirectly questioned her competence. Frilly, light-colored, and sexy skirts are twice as likely as conservative dark skirts to elicit a negative response from women executives. Only a handful of the women managers, executives, and professionals reacted like men and instinctively questioned the wearer's competence or dedication when she wears a conservative skirt; the majority questioned only her business savvy. However, they have been conditioned by a male-dominated business environment and are likely to treat a woman wearing a tight, short, or light- or bright-colored skirt as an inferior.

Looking as if it is part of a conservative traditional suit will not guarantee that a skirt will send an executive message. It must also look rich, and that usually means 100 percent wool. Although a number of materials tested well, including some man-made fibers, only skirts made of wool or that looked as if they were sent positive massages consistently. In warm weather skirts made of linen or looking as if they were also send positive messages. Today a number of artificial fibers are as rich and good-looking as wool, but unless you have developed upper-middle-class taste I recommend 100 percent wool models.

When buying a skirt, you must consider a number of factors. The most important, particularly if you intend to wear the skirt without a jacket, is how it will stand up to wear. Avoid any skirt that clings, rides up, or wrinkles. The fact that materials like linen breathe and are comfortable shouldn't convince you to purchase them, unless they are wrinkle resistant. In most cases a woman in a linen skirt looks as though she has been sleeping in it after only a few hours. The advantage of artificial fibers and blends is that they keep their shape and fresh look for hours. Unfortunately you cannot always tell by reading the content label how easily a skirt will wrinkle; you have to test it. You test a skirt the same way you do a suit: grab the material, hold it in your hand for at least ten seconds, and let go. If the wrinkles do not disappear immediately, reject the skirt.

Good skirts, like good suits, are never cut skimpily. A skimpy cut is usually the sign of a second-rate skirt. Check to see if a skirt has an ample hem and there is enough material in the seams to allow for minor adjustments. Keep in mind that you can raise or lower hems only so much because most skirts are designed to be worn at a certain length. The cut of the skirt and the position of buttons, zippers, or pockets limit how much you can move the hemline of most skirts.

No matter what fashion says, you should never wear miniskirts to work. Many women look at miniskirts and see fashion and think businesslike; most men look at miniskirts, see legs, and think sex. No amount of rationalizing or name calling will change that. I have been researching skirt length since the early 1970s and have run a survey on an average of once a year. I have tested the reaction to skirt lengths in dresses, suits, skirts, and uniforms, and in twenty years nothing has changed. Short skirts do not work. At work your skirt should always be at or below your knee. Even in offices where everyone is wearing minis and some women can get away wearing a skirt an inch above the knee, I do not recommend it. Shorter skirts simply send the wrong message.

There are two additional hallmarks of quality in a skirt. First, it is reinforced at the waist. Skirts that are not are often baggy and don't hang well. Second, the zipper on a quality skirt is always concealed. In most good skirts the zipper is concealed in the seam.

Naturally, whenever you buy a skirt or any other garment, make sure it looks good on you, not on a six-foot, 110-pound model. The average woman, particularly if she is short, heavy, or hippy, should use a wraparound mirror to look at a skirt she is considering buying. We found women who were a size twelve or above and shorter than five six usually did not test well in long skirts. A skirt that says chic on a five-foot-ten, 110-pound model often says chunky and dumpy on the average woman. Short women, of course, should never wear long skirts, and no businesswoman can wear a tight skirt without destroying her professional image.

PANTS

If you want to wear the pants in the office, don't wear pants *to* the office. Our latest research shows 6 percent of men are threatened, while 53 percent admit to being turned on by women wearing pants. Some women think of pants as a masculine garment and find it hard to believe that men are sexually aroused by women in pants that are not skintight. Thin models wearing pants may not turn men on, but women with well-rounded feminine figures do. Most women understand this is dangerous, because if you turn a man on, you diminish your image as an expert or an authority figure.

For reasons I cannot even guess, men from blue-collar backgrounds are often antagonistic to women wearing pants. I did not make this discovery. Women in a number of fields whose jobs required they get the cooperation of blue-collar men had a "no pants" rule long before John T. Molloy appeared on the scene. For example, women reporters who worked the crime beat on a number of papers were told by their editors not to wear pants, because those who had gone before them found that when they wore pants it was far more difficult to get the police to cooperate with them.

It is not just men from blue-collar backgrounds who react negatively to women in pants; men from all backgrounds are less likely to listen to or cooperate with women in pants. Ann, who is now a partner in one of America's most prestigious law firms, developed a skin condition when she was thirty-two and wore long sleeves and pants for almost three years. She was a very bright young attorney whose career was about to take off when the rash spread to her legs. Ann said the minute she put on pants she had difficulty dealing with male partners, associates, and judges. From that point on she had to fight twice as

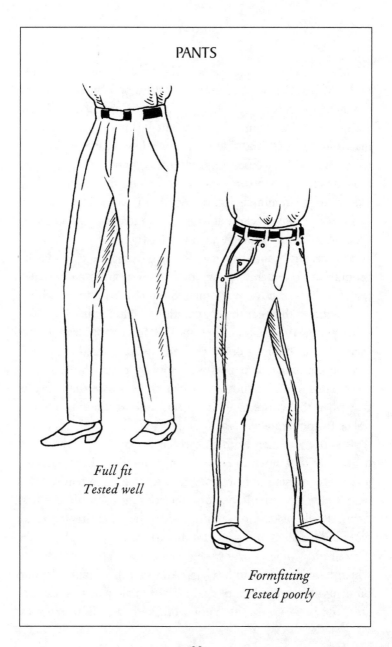

PANTS

Full fit
Tested well

Formfitting
Tested poorly

hard for everything. When the condition cleared up she changed not only firms, but states. She felt she needed a fresh start if she was to succeed. What made Ann's story so important is that I hear it over and over from well-educated women who regularly wore pants.

Although I advise women not to wear pants to work, I realize some women must. They work at jobs where they have to climb up, under, and over things, and it is simply not practical for them to wear a dress or skirt. If you must wear pants, you should follow these guidelines. One, choose a cut and style that deemphasizes your feminine figure. Loose and full-cut styles work best. Two, wear dark colors. Three, stick to solids; they are safest. Some very traditional and conservative patterns like subtle plaids and herringbone checks did test well, but not as well as solids. Four, if practical, wear a jacket with your pants, preferably one that hangs at least six inches below your waist. The obvious choice is a blazer, but any jacket that camouflages the shape of your hips and waist will do. Five, never wear blue jeans; women never look effective in blue jeans.

Please note I said blue jeans. Denim pants dyed khaki, beige, brown, and black will work for women when their male counterparts wear blue jeans. Because so many women in factories insist on wearing blue jeans, I tested them. The ones that worked best were loose fitting, even baggy. Those without traditional metal fasteners or leather labels tested best.

An ideal pair of women's slacks designed for leisure wear fit snugly at the hips, waist, and seat, while an ideal pair of slacks designed for business should fit snugly only at the waist. With both pairs the legs should fall without puckering, and the pants should fall to the design length. Pants designed to hang above the ankle, or of materials that adhere to the shape of a woman's leg, do not test well. The pants that worked best had a traditional pleated cut that allowed them to look neat without clinging to the wearer when she is standing or sitting.

When I suggest putting a jacket on over pants, I am not advocating the return of the old polyester pantsuit or anything that resembles it. If you must wear pants, wear a tailored blazer with them.

If you have to wear pants when in the field, you should try not to wear them back to the office, even if it means carrying an extra outfit with you. Many sophisticated women who regularly have to go into the field where pants are required wear a jumpsuit that they remove before returning to the office.

Many of my client corporations supply their women with jumpsuits with company logos, and others supply them with appropriate jackets when they have to go into the field or onto the factory floor. In several companies, being issued a company jumpsuit or jacket has become a status symbol, derived from the fact that only women managers or engineers regularly go into the field or onto the factory floor. To be practical and effective, jumpsuits and jackets must fit loosely so they can be worn over a variety of outfits. One word of caution: These company outfits should be cleaned as soon as they become stained or rumpled looking. In spite of the fact that these outfits are being used to protect the wearer's clothing in situations where getting dirty is almost a given, if a woman dons a poorly kept model, she will lose some of her authority.

The best colors for a businesswoman's pants are navy, black, gray, beige with a touch of gray in it, dark brown, and bluish gray. The worst colors are bright, light, and pastel. The one exception to this rule is white. Well-tailored white and off white pants are perfectly acceptable at company outings. Most other colors do not work. Every shade of red, orange, lavender, green, yellow, pink, and mustard we tested failed.

VESTS

To keep up with the times, I have changed my advice on suits, jackets, and most other garments. However, the reason I have changed my advice on wearing vests is that when I researched the original *Woman's Dress for Success Book*, I made a mistake.

The vests that were being pushed by the fashion industry at the time and the only ones being shown in stores in New York, where I was located, were designed to accentuate a woman's bust. They acted almost like the WonderBra. They pushed up a woman's breasts and made her appear bustier. The minute the book appeared on the shelves I received an avalanche of complaints from very intelligent, articulate, and successful businesswomen throughout the country. They insisted that vests did not send a negative message but were a very effective and useful business garment. Naturally I immediately retested.

Those women were right: vests could help a businesswoman's image. Wearing a vest in an office where the men took off their jackets allowed the women to relax their dress and fit in with their male co-workers without losing authority. When a woman wore a vest the same color as her skirt, a majority of the businesspeople we interviewed assumed that she had a suit jacket somewhere. Since the suit is a power uniform in most businesses, wearing a vest put women on a more equal footing with men.

This was a very important finding. When we showed one hundred men and women pictures of men wearing slacks that looked as if they could be part of a suit, then asked them if the wearer had a suit jacket hanging somewhere, 91 percent said yes. This is significant, because most people assume suit wearers are better educated and more likely to be in charge than nonsuit wearers. When we showed pictures of a woman wearing a skirt that looked as if it might be part of a suit, only 31 percent of those questioned assumed she was a suit wearer; the rest assumed she was neither well educated nor in a position of authority.

Women, particularly in male-dominated fields like engineering, felt they had to go along with casual male dress codes. I interviewed dozens of bright, able women who said when they wore jackets while their male co-workers were in shirtsleeves, they were kidded about their dress. A majority of the women who experienced this so-called kidding chose to leave their jackets home even though they knew they were less likely to be treated like professionals without them. The discovery that when a woman wore a vest that matched her skirt she could take off her jacket and maintain a professional image solved a major problem of women working in shirtsleeve offices.

Most vests, including ones that do not match the wearer's skirt, add to a woman's authority and professionalism. The more traditional vests worked best. They were cut so they fit snugly but did not look as if they were sprayed on. Interestingly, the oversize Annie Hall vests worked no better than the very tight models. They made some women look like little girls dressed up in Daddy's clothing, which is too cute and too sexy for the office. Sweater vests and those made of frilly or sexy material also made the wearer appear less effective.

Unfortunately, today not many women's suits come with vests. A number of women executives in high-tech fields have their suits made so they can get a matching vest. When I heard what they were doing, I thought they would regret spending hundreds of dollars just to get a vest. However, when I interviewed these women they said that a vest was a worthwhile investment. The vest can be a wonderful garment for a woman when she is in an environment where a suit jacket or a regular jacket can't be worn comfortably.

SWEATERS

Sweaters are not part of the uniform of executive and professional women. When a woman wears a sweater she often sends a sexual message. In the office a woman who sends a sexual message is not seen as a serious businessperson. If the thermostat in your office is set low and you are cold, put on a jacket, not a sweater.

Keep in mind that sweaters are great seduction garments. If you want to seduce your boss, it is terrific (particularly if you have a nice shape). It sends a very soft, feminine, seductive message. The one exception to this rule are sweaters that are a cross between a sweater and a blouse, worn under suits by women who are not particularly busty. Traditional blouses work better, but sweater blouses are perfectly acceptable. The ones that worked best were in rich subdued colors and were loose fitting. However, even women who can wear a knit garment in place of a blouse with a suit cannot remove their jackets and maintain their professional image.

SCARVES

Scarves are part of the business uniform for some women. Large scarves draped over one shoulder are worn by executive and professional women in all sections of the country. Several years ago, when the look was popular and fashionable, more women wore scarves than they do today, but a number of women continue to wear them to business.

A majority of the male executives we surveyed thought a woman with a rich scarf draped over her shoulders was an aggressive, successful businesswoman. About ten years ago the

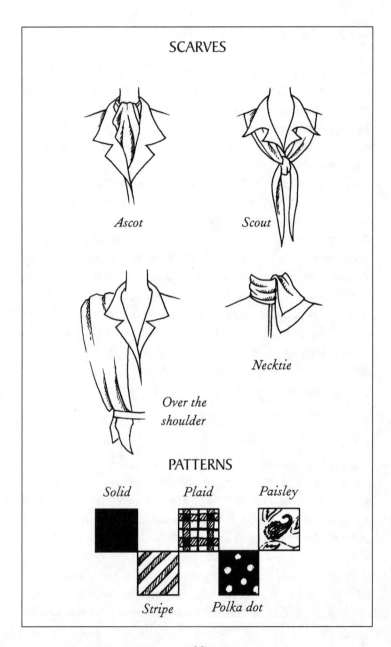

SCARVES

Ascot

Scout

Over the shoulder

Necktie

PATTERNS

Solid   *Plaid*   *Paisley*

Stripe   *Polka dot*

scarf became an optional part of the executive and professional woman's work uniform, and it remains so today, even though the look is not as fashionable as it once was.

To be effective these scarves usually have to be obviously expensive. The best scarves scream money. Although most men can't tell a good scarf from a poor one, they instinctively know a scarf that adds status to the wearer. We showed a group of executives pictures of the same woman wearing a neutral navy dress with a very expensive and an obviously inexpensive scarf draped over her shoulder and asked what each did for a living. A majority of the men and over 80 percent of the women thought the woman with the expensive scarf was an executive or professional and the woman with the inexpensive scarf was a clerk or secretary. Because scarves (like most accessories) either scream money, power, and ability or secretarial pool, no one can afford a cheap one.

If you are not sure which scarves scream money and class, you are probably choosing the wrong ones. Your best bet is to buy designer scarves in the very best store in town, but not just any designer scarf. Seek out an experienced saleslady and enlist her help. Ask her to point out expensive designer scarves that have been selling for years. If you are not sure which patterns work, choose the patterns and colors found in traditional men's ties—paisley, foulards, and so on. Don't pinch pennies when purchasing a scarf. Scarves, like most accessories, should be looked upon as investments. It is wise to buy the best.

FOOTWEAR

I regularly give a slide presentation on dressing for success. The only slide that I used twenty years ago that I still use is a picture of six conservative pumps. I tell the audience I used this picture in research twenty-five years ago, and although the heels on today's pumps are slimmer, nothing else has changed. The executive slipper for a businesswoman remains a traditional closed heel, closed toe pump in a conservative color with one-and-a-half- to two-inch heels. While a businesswoman can wear brighter, lighter colors in suits and jackets, she is still better off if she wears a simple pump in conservative colors.

The colors that test best haven't really changed in twenty years. They remain navy, medium blue, black, deep brown, gray, maroon, brown, tan, beige, and cordovan. In the summer and in the Sun Belt you can get away with lighter colors, but even there they do not test as well as darker models.

This is one case where you cannot play follow the leader. Many successful women, even some who admit that dark shoes work and are more businesslike, often choose to wear lighter colors and more casual styles. For example, almost one-third of the executive and professional women who videotaped their shoes as part of their personal video consultation this year, owned at least one pair of white pumps, while almost half had at least one pair of pastel pumps. You can wear lighter-colored pumps if you obey one rule: Do not wear brightly colored pumps, pumps with loud ornaments, or pumps in unusual colors.

The most common mistake made by women is to wear shoes that match bright or light color outfits. They would look more professional if they wore a darker shade of the same color.

Boots do not work in business. Every couple of years the fashion industry brings them back and tells women that they can wear boots to work. It is not so; even the most conservative boots do not work very well. If you work in a northern climate and are forced to walk through sleet and snow, you can wear boots to the office, but you must take them off the minute you arrive. The fact that you do not wear them in the office does not make their color or design any less important. Boots— even those you wear only to the office—must be conservative in cut and color. The best colors are brown and black, followed by most shades of tan.

Open-toed or sling-back shoes or shoes with very high or spiked heels also tested poorly. Open-toed and sling-back shoes are either too informal or too dressy for the office, and high heels on most women send a very sexy message.

Short women can benefit from wearing high heels, since these may increase their sense of presence and authority. However, since wearing high heels arches a woman's back and gives her a very sexy look, short women should wear fully cut jackets when wearing high heels. Avoid the extremes in footwear design, particularly shoes with very high heels or very pointy toes. They can ruin your feet and your career at the same time.

Wearing running shoes or walking shoes to work has become almost a hallmark of working women in some large cities (New York, Chicago, Los Angeles). While three years ago I advised strongly against it, I no longer do. You can get away with wearing running shoes to work, if most of the executive and professional women in your office wear them. I use the term "get away with it" because that is exactly what you will be doing. There remains a small percentage of men and women who think wearing walking shoes to the office is inappropriate. They will think less of you if you do. Before you decide whether to wear walking shoes to work, ask your boss and other key people what they think.

Many women wear walking shoes to work or cloddy shoes at work because they want to be comfortable. I do not think that is a valid reason for wearing unacceptable footwear. I surveyed over a hundred women in New York City, Chicago, and Los Angeles and asked them if they had pumps they considered very comfortable. Twenty-two of them picked the pump called Easy Spirit—the model advertised on television, worn by women playing basketball. Apparently the pump is structured much like a walking shoe. It gives a woman support as well as (apparently) some comfort. If your aim is comfort, try Easy Spirit or one of several similar pumps.

PANTY HOSE

Today women have a bit more leeway on what type of panty hose they can wear to the office. Flesh-colored ones continue to test best. We found that black and navy blue panty hose work with matching dresses and suits, but only on thin young women.

Mesh panty hose and patterned panty hose should never be worn for business. The only profession in which you are likely to succeed when wearing them is the oldest one.

HATS

In 1974 in the original book I told businesswomen that they could wear feminine fedoras. They still work; however, with the exception of Hillary Clinton, the queen of England, and half a dozen other women, businesswomen don't wear hats. They find putting them on and taking them off is too much of a hassle. They were very popular for a while, but they have almost disappeared from the business scene.

When we surveyed women who own hats, we found that they wore them half a dozen times and then left them home. If you haven't purchased one, save your money.

GLOVES

The best gloves for a businesswoman are leather or suede. The colors that work best are brown, dark brown, tan, black, and gray. Most other gloves test poorly.

If you are dressing for a social occasion, leather works, but you can also wear any material that gives a softer and feminine look. Obviously tight gloves can make a woman's hands look very attractive, and long gloves can add a touch of formality to most outfits.

When you purchase gloves you have to keep in mind what you are going to do with them. It is important to remember, if you live in a cold area, that the fingers should be lined as well as the hands because the fingers get cold first. (By the way, although mittens are inappropriate for business, they will keep your hands warmer than gloves.)

COATS

A coat is by its nature an investment garment. For the last seventy years the same four or five classic designs have been in style, and a well-made coat will last at least ten years.

The best winter coats are made of wool and are in neutral colors that go with almost anything. I conducted personal consultations after speaking at three conventions in the New York City area last winter. I asked the participants to bring their out-

erwear with them, and I brought a tailor. Before the participants arrived, he looked at their coats and estimated the cost of
manufacture and the fair retail price of each garment.

When we asked the women where they had bought their
coats and how much they paid for them, we made several dis-
coveries. The best coats were bought in major department
stores and the women's departments of traditional men's
stores. Some with designer names were worth every penny
they had paid, and some were vastly overpriced. The best
stores were the safest place to buy. They were pricey, but most
of the coats were well made. However, if you know what you
are doing, you can shop in Macy's and J. C. Penney and for a
fraction of the price get coats that are every bit as good as those
found in the most expensive stores.

If you are a top professional or executive, need a status coat,
and would not consider wearing fur, you should purchase an
overcoat made of vicuña, cashmere, a good faux fur, or some
other expensive material. When you are making that type of
investment a top store is the only place to shop. Keep in mind
that black and navy look luxurious and will go with a number
of outfits but may show every speck of dust, which makes
them impractical. You should also pass on any material that
seems to attract every dust particle in the vicinity. Some cash-
meres have this property.

Women can wear most light or bright colors if the coat is
conservatively cut, but I do not recommend them. Traditional
male business colors are more useful because they send a more
effective message about the wearer and go with more garments.
A camel or light gray wraparound made of a good wool are the
two coats that tested best. They announced that the wearer was
both authoritative and professional. If you are more than a few
pounds over your ideal weight, do not choose a wraparound

BEST WINTER COAT

Camel-colored wraparound

model; it will add weight. There are a wide selection of materials and styles that work, but most often traditional, conservative coats tested better.

There are three rules for coats. It cannot look tight or skimpy. Most of the coats that tested poorly were owned by women who gained weight and continued to wear, if not the same coat, the same size coat. About 20 percent of the women whose dress size increased made this mistake in spite of the fact that they would never consider wearing a tight suit or dress. If you have gained weight recently, look at yourself in a wraparound mirror the next time you are in a store. You may find out it is time for a new coat.

Length is another factor you must consider. Short coats do not work. Even if they have been designed to be short, you should not wear them to work. If you own a car coat or a bomber jacket, leave it home. A winter coat should be long enough to cover whatever you are going to wear under it.

If you own several winter coats, one of them should be designed to wear with a floor-length dress. That is the one time it is not necessary for your coat to cover your dress, but it should come close. We ran a test in the Crown Center Hotel in Kansas City twenty years ago that I repeated in New York last year. We stood our respondents outside a formal dance and asked them to comment on the dress of the women attending. It was winter, and most were wearing a coat over a formal dress. We identified the women as employees of a firm and asked the respondents to guess what positions they held and how much they earned. On both occasions the length of the women's coats counted more than age. The women wearing longer coats were invariably identified as executives, while the women wearing coats just below the knee were most often described as low-level employees. The responses were so predictable that my researchers dubbed short coats worn over long dresses "the peasant formal."

The best raincoat is a belted model in beige. While that is the only color that works for men, women can wear any conservative color, including black. Women's raincoats can also be cut fuller and be made of a variety of materials. They work equally well when they are single- or double-breasted, with or without belts and buckles and epaulets. Businesswomen's raincoats work if they keep the wearer dry and are not too busy, too cute, too casual, too kookie, or too trendy. Of course, to be practical a raincoat must hang at least three inches below the knee. Any model that is made of slicker material or any shiny finish can create problems. Once again it is safest to stick to the basics.

I continue to advise against wearing fur coats to business or business functions because the fur war continues unabated. In 1974 about 3 percent of the population objected to people wearing furs. By the early 1980s they did not count because in some companies the women had adopted the mink as an executive status symbol. If a woman who had not reached the executive ranks showed up wearing a mink, she might be told to leave it home until she earned the right. By the late 1980s the antifur people had launched a very successful campaign against wearing furs. Not all women left their furs at home, but a substantial percentage did, most because they were intimidated. Lately I have noticed more women wearing furs to work, so I ran several focus groups. At present the antifur people have grown to about 7 percent and are as adamant as ever. Although the fur wearers outnumber them three to one and are annoyed by the antifur people's attempt to intimidate them, I still think

RAINWEAR

Best raincoat style

it is too dangerous to wear furs. I am sure furs kill more deals than they help make, and the first rule of dressing for success is to never let your clothing get in the way of business.

LEATHER ENVELOPES, PORTFOLIOS, BRIEFCASES, AND ATTACHÉ CASES

A briefcase, a generic term for all of the above, is one of the hallmarks of an executive or professional woman. Add it to your wardrobe and you add status. We ran a test with sixty-one women who carried briefcases on alternate days and reported how it affected their treatment. They said it was particularly useful when they were dressed casually and when they were on the road. They received better treatment from waiters, desk clerks, and other service personnel when carrying briefcases. Apparently carrying one announced to strangers that they were businesswomen with some stature.

All of the briefcases worked, but as expected, expensive ones worked better. While a leather briefcase that cost $65 impressed desk clerks and bellboys, it took one that cost several hundred to impress most executives and the maître d's in better restaurants. Only seven of the sixty-one women owned a designer or other obviously expensive briefcase before participating in this test, but nine had purchased one thirty days after the test was completed and sixteen more were considering doing the same. Forty-four said they thought buying a very good briefcase was a good investment and said if they needed one in the future, they would invest in a good one. Forty-nine said if they had a daughter starting in business, they would buy her a good briefcase. The women who tested them were convinced spending money on a briefcase was an investment in their careers, and they convinced me and I hope you.

While many top executive men carry simple leather envelopes, they are carried by only a few women, with good reason. Men carrying them were usually identified as executives, while women carrying them were most often identified as executive assistants, secretaries, or saleswomen. They added no status to women, probably because any leather bag a woman clutches under her arm becomes a pocketbook.

The favorite of top women executives and professionals is the portfolio. It is nothing more than two or more connected leather envelopes with a handle and/or a shoulder strap. The women we spoke to said they preferred them because they were soft sided and light. Professional women who have to carry more papers than fit comfortably into a portfolio usually carry briefcases that are a bit larger and attaché cases that are hard sided and much larger. Unless you are an attorney you should avoid attaché cases so large that they look as if they belong to a man. Women attorneys can get away with very large bags because they have to carry files into court. The two most successful women attorneys we interviewed both carried their files in a Coach briefcase that looks like and can carry as many papers as an old-fashioned school bag.

After several sessions of the telephone tag team, we came up with the following suggestions:

1. Never buy a cheap model. Plastic, vinyl, and most cloth bags look cheap. Expensive tweed sometimes works, but nylon seldom does.

2. A briefcase should not look masculine. Don't buy one that is too big.

3. Play follow the leader. If your company or your industry

expects someone at your level to carry a certain type of bag, you must do so. In about one company in four there is an unwritten rule about what type of bag to carry. In one financial company most of the women in management carry Gucci briefcases, while in another a majority of the vice presidents carry Mark Cross briefcases. Many women are outraged when they hear this, but they shouldn't be. All it means is that women in power are, in subtle ways, controlling how those around them look. Male executives have been doing this for years.

If you work in a business where individuality is prized, the way to play follow the leader is to look different but not too different. Most women who work in the media, publishing, advertising, and similar industries work so hard at being individuals that they end up looking very different from women in middle American industries and the same as the women in their industries. All businesses have dress codes.

4. You should own a standard brown or tan briefcase before you buy an exotic color or design.

5. You can carry one with a pocketbook, if it is the right pocketbook. Don't carry a matched set; it is usually too much.

6. A briefcase is an investment, so you can spend more for quality. A good one will last at least ten years, if you take care of it.

7. Don't fill your briefcase with personal items. Sooner or later you will open it and they will pour out. Remember, Murphy was an optimist. The most embarrassing items will spill out at the most inopportune time, in front of the most important people.

8. Bring all the papers you need on a busy day when you go to buy a briefcase and see if they fit. This may lead you to conclude, like several of the women who took part in the research, that the design of the inside of the case is more important than the design of the outside.

9. Do not buy a $1,500 ostrich briefcase to impress people who would not know an ostrich case if they fell over it. The most effective status symbols are the ones that can be spotted by the average man across a large room.

10. Never overfill a briefcase, especially a soft-sided one. Most women agree that if it bulges, it loses its executive style.

11. Never buy one that could be mistaken by the most unsophisticated person for an oversize pocketbook. A briefcase must be very businesslike.

12. Never have your name engraved on the outside of a briefcase or any other item. It can make you a target.

13. Never buy one with a key lock; keys, especially those small ones, get misplaced. A dial lock is the better choice.

HANDBAGS

The best handbags for a businesswoman to carry are obviously expensive satchel bags with a handle and optional shoulder strap. There is no standard size or design, but the ones that tested best were nine inches wide, five inches tall, and three inches deep, with neat, squared-off corners and clean, understated hardware. The best material for any handbag is leather. There are designer bags made of vinyl that work because the logos that cover them announce that they are expensive and give them a certain status. However, even among the designer bags the best ones are made of leather.

The best colors are brown, beige, black, and navy, but others work as well. Pastel and bright-colored handbags do not send a business message, nor do handbags that are too dressy. Beige or light tan are better summer colors than white, but you can carry a white handbag if it has a businesslike design and is

BUSINESS STYLES

Handbag

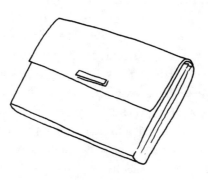

Leather envelope

in perfect condition. Unfortunately white bags, even good ones, begin to look a bit shabby almost as soon as you break them in, and no businesswoman should ever carry a handbag that even begins to look worn around the edges.

Since 1990 I enlisted three groups of executive and professional women to test different handbags. They said that when they carried large, feminine, dressy, or inexpensive handbags they were not treated with as much respect as when they carried business models. They also agreed that just about anyone could tell which handbags were appropriate for business and which were not. At first most of the women bought designer handbags since they were spending so much for them, but many were not happy with them. One problem that occurred again and again was that the shoulder straps on very expensive handbags fell apart when the bag still looked new and the manufacturer wanted over a hundred dollars for a replacement.

After less than two years in the study most of the women decided that good leather bags were the way to go. A small minority solved the problem of shoddy overpriced designer bags by buying knock-offs for as little as one-twentieth of the regular price; when I asked them if they felt guilty, they said not after having a five- or six-hundred-dollar designer bag fall apart in less than two seasons. I suspect for everyone who admitted doing this, only two or three actually engaged in the practice. Some of the knock-offs bought in flea markets and on street corners in New York, Chicago, and Los Angeles, while lacking quality, looked identical to the genuine articles and tested just as well.

In the 1970s carrying a handbag made a businesswoman look less effective, particularly if she carried it with a briefcase. Today a businesslike handbag is part of the uniform of most executive and professional women and can be carried everywhere. Every businesswoman should have half a dozen in her wardrobe.

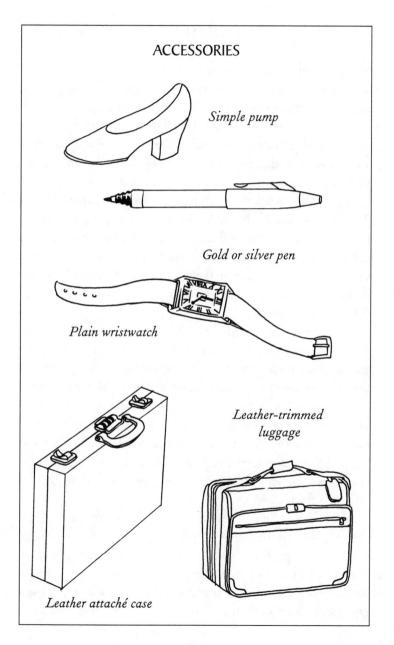

ACCESSORIES

Simple pump

Gold or silver pen

Plain wristwatch

Leather-trimmed luggage

Leather attaché case

WALLETS

The best wallets are designer models. These have a status that even a good leather wallet does not have. As strange as it sounds, people are more impressed if you pull a designer wallet out of a good leather bag than if you pull out a matching leather wallet. Matching leather wallets work, but since most women do not change their wallets when they change bags, your wallet does not have to match your bag.

The most useful thing about any wallet is what is in it. That's right: the credit cards. Businesswomen should have at least two, a bank card and an American Express card. If you can get one, a gold or platinum American Express card can be very useful for a woman on the way up. It announces to people that you have already achieved some success, and that is a useful message to send.

When you are on the road or entertaining at a strange restaurant you can avoid the embarrassment of having the waiter give the check to your male guest by signaling him that you are the one paying. The easiest way to do this is to place a credit card on the table in plain sight. Of course, you should not have to do this when you are at home because every businesswoman should have one restaurant where she is known as a big tipper and as a result is treated like visiting royalty. This allows you to entertain and impress your guests seemingly without effort.

We sent women into restaurants in different outfits to test if their dress made a difference. It does; if you are dressed like an executive or professional, you will receive better treatment than you will when you are dressed like a housewife or secretary. However, clothing, no matter how good, will not get you equal treatment with most men. Maître d's, waiters, and waitresses told us that women, no matter what they claim, do not tip as well as men. Many women tip well only when they are spending the company's money. These women make the mistake of going to the same restaurant where they entertain clients and leaving an inadequate gratuity. Naturally, when they return with clients they are treated shabbily. You should have one restaurant where you always overtip; it is the only way of guaranteeing good service every time.

ALL OTHER GARMENTS

If you are not sure, buy the most expensive, traditional model and you will be right 80 percent of the time.

Chapter Five

Dressing for the Job

Obviously, if you don't have a job, you can't dress for your job. So I will begin with dressing for a job interview. I have been researching this subject for almost thirty years, and fifteen years ago I conducted a major research project in this area. At that time I was speaking at colleges and universities, and students kept asking me how they should dress for job interviews. I felt I needed more data before advising these students. The resulting research uncovered three basic truths.

1. Proper dress is almost never a reason for landing a job — but that does not make it unimportant. Improper dress is the most common reason job candidates are eliminated.
2. A woman's dress counts more than a man's, particularly when she is being interviewed by another woman.
3. Three times as many women as men are turned down because of how they are dressed.

In 1994 I updated this research. My researchers interviewed 384 men and women who regularly hire people and had hired at least four people in the last year. We asked them not only how they thought a candidate should dress, but how the candidates who were successful dressed and how the candidates who were unsuccessful dressed. About 75 percent of those interviewed were human resources people, but I also interviewed three presidents of companies and headhunters who specialized in different industries and came from different sections of the United States.

This research uncovered a number of additional factors important to women:

1. The best look for interviewing is conservative chic. The outfit that tested best with the people who hired college graduates consisted of a pricey, conservatively but not traditionally cut, medium-range blue wool suit, a traditionally cut white silk blouse, skin-toned panty hose, navy pumps, and, for jewelry, an expensive but not flashy gold chain.

2. All industries and most companies have official or unofficial dress codes. If you look as though you would fit in, you improve your chances of being hired.

3. Looking attractive helps; looking beautiful does not.

4. If you are interviewed by a man, you increase your chances of getting the job if you wear "male" business colors.

5. Interviewers who are women respond best to women who mirror their image.

6. Interview clothing should be used to help create an overall impression. If you are outgoing and tend to be exuberant, use your conservative clothing to modify your message. Similarly, if you are shy and introverted, wear clothing with pizzazz. When we took candidates with these image challenges and changed their clothing, we changed their message and improved their success rate.

Dressing for the Job

The information in the remainder of the chapter on the proper dress for doctors, lawyers, managers, accountants, and others is based on research in companies that hire a substantial number of people in these professions. The section on accountants, secretaries, and managers is based on interviews with people in these fields, including managers and executives who make decisions about hiring and promoting. We conducted in-depth interviews with at least one hundred people in each field in five different locations and different companies. In most cases we interviewed far more than one hundred people and included the key decision makers. In addition, we received 1,164 internal reviews. Each of these reviews had a special section in which the executive conducting the review was required to make a comment about the appearance or image of the person being reviewed. In a number of companies we were able to look at the same person's review over a number of years and check the correlation between image and advancement.

I could fill several chapters with just the information on lawyers and salespeople. I have spent hundreds of thousands of hours over the past thirty years interviewing people in these fields. For many years I have interviewed not only lawyers, judges, and juries, but also the people who worked in courtrooms, and I've asked them if they could spot a successful lawyer. In addition, I interviewed law firm partners who determined which young lawyers were to be promoted. I am currently writing a book on sales, and, of course, the information on dressing to sell is based on the research done for that book, which includes ten thousand hours of videotapes of salespeople in actual sales situations and follow-up interviews with both the buyer and seller.

That is why you will find in this chapter detailed advice, which varies depending on your company, your field, where you live, and the appropriate "uniform" of the people you work for and with. More hours of research and more information is contained in this chapter than was in the entire original *Woman's Dress for Success Book*.

I hope you find it useful.

HOW TO DRESS FOR AN INTERVIEW

If you are being interviewed by a man, it is best to dress as if you already have the job and have even received two promotions. We showed male lawyers pictures of women and said they were applying for secretarial positions. The women they identified as the most qualified candidates were dressed like lawyers. Most wore suits or similar outfits.

Men in other professions based their decisions on the same logic. Women applying for clerical positions who were interviewed by men fared far better if they wore jacket outfits, even if a dress was a uniform for secretaries.

Men chose women who dressed one or two steps above the job they were seeking. When we asked the men why they made the choice they did, they said they were getting a bargain. As they saw it, they were paying for a secretary but getting someone a lot better qualified.

Female interviewers do not react this way. They expect a woman to dress for the job for which she is applying. They want secretaries to look like secretaries, lawyers to look like lawyers, and managers to look like managers. It is not that they do not favor candidates who dress up; they do. Women interviewers are most likely to hire women who are dressed in the best version of the look worn by women who already have the job.

Ideally, if you are applying for a job, it would be best if you dressed in an outfit that would be suitable for the job and also suitable if you received a promotion. In firms where the secretaries regularly wear jackets, a jacket outfit will give you an advantage.

When applying for a clerical position, wear either a skirt and blouse with a jacket over it, or a dress with a jacket over it. Both the skirt and blouse or the dress should be in a traditional color. I do not recommend wearing navy or black—these colors are too powerful—nor do I advise bright red, which is just a bit too flashy for a job interview. A beige jacket over a blue dress is ideal because it is formal without being executive and conservative without being drab. In the 1970s men responded best to women in suits applying for clerical positions, but the suit has become so associated with women in management and professional positions that it no longer is appropriate for women applying for administrative and other support positions.

The best colors to wear when applying for nonadministrative positions are medium-range blue, either as a dress or a jacket, or beige, either as a dress or a jacket. There is no magic formula.

These color selections do not apply if you are being interviewed by a woman. While they will not turn off the interviewer, they are not as effective as outfits that because of their color or cut are just a touch more feminine.

Do not confuse feminine with glamorous or sexy—these looks are interview killers. It is significant that the most common negative comment made by both male and female interviewers about women they turned down is that they wore too much makeup or perfume.

After looking at the research, the woman who was in charge of hiring for a Fortune 500 company sighed and said, "John, you know what you have discovered? . . . My mother was right. She told me when applying for a job, dress as if you were going to church with your boyfriend. You should look attractive but not sexy." I do not think her mother's simplistic formula would work in every case, but she did understand the most effective message for an applicant to send is: "I am a reliable, trustworthy, decent person." Isn't that whom everyone would like to hire?

Blue-Collar Jobs

If a woman is applying for a traditional male job that requires her to get her hands dirty, she cannot dress in the same way she would if she were applying for a white-collar job. One of the most important messages that your clothing has to send is that you are ready, willing, and able to perform the physical functions of the job.

In spite of the progress women have made in the workplace, the prejudice against women performing what used to be male jobs is still very strong. For those job interviews you will do better if you are dressed in nonfeminine colors. Don't wear anything pink or frilly.

Both men and women doing the hiring rejected women who came looking too cute, too delicate, too feminine, or too sexy. The perfect example of that is when we showed pictures of women in four types of makeup—heavy, chic, average, and minimal—to people hiring women in the construction industry. Forty-nine percent picked the women with the least amount of makeup, 42 percent chose the woman with average makeup, and only 9 percent, all of whom were men, picked the women with heavy makeup. Both the men and the women told us that they had hired women who stayed around for a couple of weeks and quit. Most of them looked as if they were dressed for a date and not a hard day's work. So when women applied for these positions wearing heavy makeup, with long nails, or dressed in a way that would make it impossible for them to do physical labor, they were not hired.

Short hair works here. If you have very long hair, even if it is tied up, it decreases your chances of being perceived as an effective person in a blue-collar environment. Long, flowing hair is the kiss of death. When we showed pictures of women with long, flowing hair to men and women who interviewed candidates for these positions, they almost invariably rejected the women.

The last person I interviewed was a woman who worked for a computer company in California. Although factory work by its nature, it was very clean, very precise factory work. Only a small percentage of those hired were required to do physical labor. Most of the women were assembling electronic components—a skill that requires attention to detail but not extraordinary physical strength.

Nevertheless the woman who did the hiring looked at our pictures and chose the women who looked as if they were ready and able to perform more strenuous tasks. When I asked her why she chose them, without realizing it she paraphrased the sixteen men and seven women I had interviewed earlier. She said that while most jobs at the plant did not require strenuous physical work, she didn't want anyone who would not be willing and able to do physical labor.

Executives and Professionals

When a woman applies for a job that requires an advanced degree or is likely to lead to a managerial position, she increases her chances of being hired if she wears a suit. If she is interviewed by a man, she should wear traditional male colors, particularly dark gray in the North and medium-range gray in the South. These colors announce to men that you are a serious businessperson.

If she is interviewed by a woman who does not wear a suit or is a fashionable dresser, she should wear a feminine suit. Many of the fashionable women we interviewed said they would eliminate a woman if she wore a dress for success suit because they think that such a woman is not self-confident. Women, as I have stated, look upon their clothing as a statement of their personality, and someone who dresses differently is telling them that they are wrong. Women in positions of power are every bit as insistent that the people they hire follow a strict dress code as are men in pinstripe suits. We saw that women repeatedly favored other women who dressed in a style that identified them as socioeconomic sisters.

The most important step any woman can take is to find out who is interviewing her. If she cannot find out, she should attempt to identify the style of executive women in that company. The easiest way to do this is to show up a day early. Make it a point to arrive before the employees in the morning or just before lunchtime. Study carefully what the executive women are wearing and adjust your outfit to mirror that style. It is a worthwhile effort.

Most women being interviewed for managerial, premanagerial, or other professional positions are interviewed by at least one other woman. Many male executives think that women can read other women much more accurately than men and assign women to interview other women.

High-Fashion Jobs

If you are being interviewed for a high-fashion company, you should wear a stylish feminine suit. Your dress should not be sexy or avant garde. People in the fashion industries, surprisingly, do not trust women who dress in sexy or outlandish styles. They react in much the same way as those in other industries—they are most likely to hire candidates who are traditional by *their* standards. With your feminine suit you need stylish, fashionable secondary garments and accessories—they will not hire anyone who looks as if she is applying for a position at IBM. They are impressed by women who look fashionable without looking trendy and whose clothes state "I have good taste." One of the best ways of achieving such a look is to purchase your entire outfit at one store. Often the stores that sell expensive, stylish feminine suits display their suits with shoes, blouses, and accessories. These outfits are usually put together by a professional with style and panache, and that is exactly what is needed in these "glamour" industries. Keep in mind that your image must be businesslike. If you go into a store that claims to be dressing executive women and the look strikes you as even moderately flamboyant, leave the store and keep shopping.

The rules change the minute you reach the infamous glass ceiling. While men have to make only minor adjustments in their wardrobe when applying for top-level management positions, women often have to change their entire look. Women successfully applying for top management can be described as "ladylike." While they wear suits, their image is soft and feminine. They strike a delicate balance between understated and conservative, feminine and fashionable.

After I discovered that very able women were being stopped

by the glass ceiling, I enlisted the help of the presidents and top executives of seventeen companies. I had them look at pictures of women applying for top positions and asked them for their first reaction to these women. Sixty-three were men and nine were women.

The women's reaction to the pictures were identical to the men's. They chose "ladylike" candidates as well, but they did not use the term "ladylike." They said that the women they chose looked as if they came from sophisticated backgrounds and would fit in. The women that both groups chose had hairstyles slightly softer and slightly longer than those of middle management. Most of the women they selected wore understated makeup, but almost as many wore makeup that would be considered too much by those interviewing for middle-management positions. It touched on voguish. Some of those chosen wore suits in traditional colors—navy, gray, and blue—but others wore conservative feminine shades such as butternut and mahogany. They favored women with almost traditional suit styles. The model that won hands down was a collarless version of the original dress for success suit. They picked women wearing white businesslike blouses that were feminine but not frilly.

The jewelry that tested best was expensive, simple, appropriate, and elegant. Two of the women chosen wore a simple string of pearls; another wore her grandmother's brooch at the neck. Three women wore obviously expensive gold chains, and the majority wore expensive watches. Two wore bracelets, but neither was the clunky, noisy type. Their look was rich, elegant, upper class, ladylike, and yet businesslike.

I think the phrase that best describes them was used by an executive vice president who was part of a management team that had just hired a woman for one of the top ten spots in a

Fortune 500 company. He said that they interviewed over thirty people and they whittled the selection down to six, all of whom were "feminine but formidable."

When we finished this study it became obvious that these women had three additional characteristics in common. More were dressed in suits. While their dress was less authoritative than women in middle management, their speech and mannerisms were more bosslike. None looked over age fifty, although at least one or two were.

ON THE JOB: ACCOUNTANTS

Twenty years ago in the original *Woman's Dress for Success Book*, I recommended three suit colors for accountants—charcoal gray, medium-range gray, and light gray—with one blouse color, white. The only change today is that I also recommend pinstripe suits.

The best look for accountants is still very conservative. Today a woman can wear blue, gray, beige—traditional male colors. This is the only field in which dressing in the original "dress for success" formula is still the sole acceptable formula.

I realize that a number of successful female accountants dress in stylish, feminine suits, and some have discarded the suit altogether. However, when we asked clients of major accounting firms to choose the accountant they would want working on their books, over 90 percent of the men and 72 percent of the women picked women dressed in the traditional blue, gray, or beige skirted suit. The suits themselves that worked best were traditionally cut, with skirts just below the knee and jackets that hung six to eight inches below the waist.

Innovation in style, touches of glamour, and elegance did not help. Some women got away with this, others didn't.

Gloria, a twenty-nine-year-old CPA with several advanced degrees, worked as a tax specialist for one of the more prestigious accounting firms in her city. She and two women friends prided themselves on not "dressing like accountants." She put time, money, and effort into being a stylish dresser.

She is gifted with an almost photographic memory. When negotiating with the Internal Revenue Service, she almost always did well because she overwhelmed them with facts. When she first started doing it she had to carry tons of books with her because every time she quoted the tax code they would ask her to show them the citation. The accounts she was dealing with were so complex that no IRS agent—or group of IRS agents and team of accountants—could settle all the differences at one meeting, so usually the meetings went on over a period of time. She often dealt with the same people in subsequent meetings. One meeting with the IRS took place a day after she had returned from vacation. She was scheduled to arrive the night before, but because of the weather she returned the morning of the meeting. She arrived wearing a dated emergency blue suit that she kept in the office, a white blouse, and no makeup and carrying her attaché case and the usual books to back up her statements. She said she caught a glimpse of herself in a storefront window, and she thought she looked frumpy and plain—"like a schoolmarm." When the session started, she started quoting tax code, as was her habit. She kept interrupting and making technical legal arguments for her side. She said a strange thing happened—no one questioned her. They assumed that she knew what she was talking about. Gloria was astounded that when her image was "dull and lifeless," her adversaries perceived her brain as sharp as a razor. So she made a point of wearing this outfit to the next three meetings. She said during subsequent meetings they treated her the same way. At one or two points her opponents questioned whether she was interpreting the law or quoting the law, but they never questioned her accuracy. Suddenly she found that she had authority backing up her facile presentation of the facts, and her job became much easier.

Gloria said she was absolutely certain that when she changed her clothing she changed the way people perceived her. She said that at the end of one session an IRS agent said, "I knew you were trouble when you walked in. Your photographic memory was no surprise." She told me, "Of course, that is ridiculous. People with photographic memories don't look any different from anyone else. However, as long as the world thinks they do, I am going to dress dull and efficient."

Claudia told us she became an accountant because her father and mother were accountants. When she graduated from school she went to work for an accounting firm, but with the determination that she would never become her parents. Her father had worked twelve- to sixteen-hour days, and her mother had worked just as hard. She was raised by a Chinese couple who acted as maid, chauffeur, and baby-sitter for her parents.

When Claudia became pregnant she immediately quit her job and didn't return to her profession until her second child entered the fifth grade. Before she went back to work she bought three dress for success suits. Once she saw the other women in the office, she was convinced her clothing was out of date. Most were wearing far more stylish clothing. Even those who wore suits wore more stylish suits. Since she had bought two blue and two gray traditional dress for success suits, she couldn't afford to purchase new outfits. She decided she would wear what she had for a few months.

At the end of six months Claudia decided that being chic wasn't for her. A number of clients requested to work with her, not knowing anything about her. To them she was a serious, conservative, traditional businesswoman. She said frankly that better-qualified women didn't impress them nearly as much. In the first six months that Claudia was there, two major clients requested that she personally handle their accounts. She thought since she had taken an eleven-year hiatus that she would never become a partner. She changed her mind not because the competition, mainly other women, were ineffective, but because most of them looked less effective. She is convinced her image gives her a tremendous advantage. She is right.

Years ago we discovered that an accountant's image had as much to do with her success as did her technical skills. Most clients have no idea what their accountants are doing. Clients trust their accountants simply because they have no choice, and therefore they seek out people who look trustworthy.

I am afraid that accounting is one field where the key to success is image, and the image that works is drab.

ON THE JOB: REPORTERS

When I wrote the original *Woman's Dress for Success Book* I did research with twenty-five female newspaper reporters. I knew them because I worked in the newspaper business and they were friends of mine.

The women agreed that the primary job of a reporter is to elicit the cooperation of the people she interviews. Most reporters agree that if they dress in a style that separates them from the people they are interviewing, it is harder to elicit cooperation. This is why the general dress code in newspapers is casual—most of the time reporters talk to Joe and Josephine Average. It is also the reason most business reporters wear suits, and entertainment beat reporters often dress in an avant garde style.

When a profession has an unofficial dress code it has come about through trial and error and is usually fairly effective. In most professions the young copy the pros—including how they dress. However, the pros do not always do it right, because in most cases the dress of the professionals is affected by their backgrounds. Years ago reporters came from limited backgrounds, so when they dressed casually they fit in with Jane on the street. Today print reporters are more sophisticated, and although they still dress casually, their style is upper middle class. Their clothing may be relaxed, but it screams money, class, education, and sophistication. Since people reporters interview are often not well educated or sophisticated, their dress makes their job harder, not easier. Most female reporters' jobs would be easier if they bought their work outfits in the same stores as the people they interview. It would send a more nonthreatening message.

The primary response of most people in responsible positions to journalists is fear. They are afraid of what journalists are going to write about them. That is why many people are defensive when being interviewed. This makes a reporter's job difficult. When you are interviewing a person, you should attempt to send them a nonverbal message that you are not going to hurt them. If you are sent to interview a businessperson, I suggest that you wear a suit, because that will identify you as a businesswoman. The person you interview will likely be much more relaxed and, therefore, willing to talk. On the other hand, if you are interviewing a cabdriver, the last thing you should wear is a jacket because that would mark you as an outsider. Many reporters dress for work without a clue about whom they are going to be dealing with that day. The assignment editor sends them wherever he pleases. After talking about this with half a dozen reporters in two different focus groups, we came to the conclusion that every female reporter should have a jacket in her car or at the office. She should wear the jacket whenever she has to deal with upper-middle-class people and leave it in her closet the rest of the time.

After having a dozen reporters test different jackets, we came to the conclusion that the best color for a woman was beige, followed by light grayish blue, brown, taupe, and tan.

Years ago, when I was a stringer for a newspaper, I worked with a young reporter known to her peers as "Bloody Mary." She earned the name because every time she wrote a piece the editor would look at it and say, "We'll have the lawyers check it." She had a wonderful gift; she was twenty-two, but she looked sixteen, innocent, and not too bright. For reasons I still can't understand, she would get hard-boiled detectives and sometimes even politicians to tell her things they wouldn't even tell their wives. Once they opened up, blood ran from the typewriter keys. She was the best investigative reporter I ever knew. I wonder if she lost her edge when she stopped looking as if she could barely hurt a fly. It is a look that works.

When I told this story at one of the focus groups for reporters, a woman in her fifties said she'd had a similar experience. She had worked for a large metropolitan newspaper, and she had two uniforms. The first was a high-power uniform she wore when she dealt with people at city hall and the leaders of industry. However, when she was sent on an assignment to dig up dirt, she said she dressed like a harried housewife. She found her harried housewife look put people at ease and opened doors. A reporter's clothing should say "I am a friend and I am harmless."

These rules do not apply to TV reporters. The public is used to seeing them dressed in suits or jackets, and any change will jeopardize their credibility.

ON THE JOB: DOCTORS

Almost nothing has changed in twenty years for doctors. The most effective garment is a white doctor's coat with a stethoscope displayed prominently in the pocket. "I'm a doctor," it says, "I'm in charge, I am going to help you, listen to me."

Last year we repeated research we originally conducted twenty years ago. We asked a number of female doctors to wear a variety of pants, skirts and blouses, and dresses under the jacket and to test their reaction with new patients. The outfits that worked best under a doctor's jacket consisted of dark skirts that hung below the knee, worn with light but not white blouses. Doctors got away with wearing dresses only when they were over forty and wore the long doctor's white coats over them.

ON THE JOB: LAWYERS

Female attorneys are my favorite clients. Most understand the impact of what they wear. Often when I consult with them I learn more than they do. The most sophisticated of them are litigators who change their clothing to suit their message. Many of them have been keeping clothing calendars even before they meet me. They keep careful records of each outfit they wear and how judges and juries respond to them.

Mary, a malpractice attorney, went one step further. After reading my first *Woman's Dress for Success Book*, she took pictures of herself in every outfit and hired college students to take a survey. Then she had them ask potential jurors a series of questions, most of which dealt with how they would respond to different arguments in different outfits. As a result, Mary wears specific outfits when she represents companies and different outfits when she represents smaller clients. She also has outfits she wears when she needs to win over women on a jury, outfits that help her make an emotional appeal, and one outfit she wears when she has to get the jury to listen to her interpretation of the law. Interestingly, Mary's calendar gave her the data to pick outfits to wear before specific judges. Since she is one of the best litigators in her town, I have no doubt she is dressing for success in her highly competitive field.

Mary's research supported my findings in three areas. Looking attractive makes most female lawyers more effective—looking beautiful makes them less effective. Women are more effective making emotional appeals when they are wearing feminine clothing, and female jurors like and trust female attorneys dressed in earth tones.

If you are like Mary and have spent years figuring out what works best for you, use the following information only as a guide. However, if you have never thought much about what you wear or are convinced that you can wear short skirts or a high-fashion look to court, read this book before you go shopping. You need it.

The main change since I wrote the original book is that the number and importance of women in the legal profession has grown tremendously. If current trends continue, women may dominate the legal profession in the twenty-first century.

Naturally, with their changing role they have changed their wardrobe.

All attorneys wear two hats. In court and when negotiating for their clients, they are salespeople, and at the office they are managers. As managers they must dress in the high-authority garb of their profession, which in most firms is a suit. When acting as salespeople, they must dress like all salespeople—to match their product, customer, and approach.

Dressing for the Judge

Most women working before judges will be appearing before male judges who come out of the political clubs. Many have sacrificed financially to become judges. They are on the bench, in part, because of the prestige. A substantial number see judgeships as the road to professional and social success. And there is one important rule to remember when appearing before them: Never challenge their authority or be disrespectful. They no longer expect women to dress in conservative suits, but you must dress professionally. Many take umbrage if a lawyer dresses in an outfit that is sexy, too cute, or too leisure-looking. They will not announce that they are ruling against you because of your dress, but they will.

While many male judges in and around large cities come from political clubs, the judges in small towns and rural areas come from country clubs. They are part of the local aristocracy. Their fathers, fathers-in-law, uncles, and, in the last couple of years, aunts were probably judges. They have learned to take women seriously but bristle at abrasive big-city types. They respond best to female lawyers who wear conservative feminine suits or jackets over conservative dresses. The image you want is friendly but professional. You can still wear a traditional dress for success suit, but it works best if it is softened with a feminine blouse or accessories.

When appearing before female judges, you must look and act like a professional. This is critical. I interviewed several female jurists, and they admitted the one thing that annoyed them was a lawyer who dressed or acted unprofessionally. Many of these judges were lawyers when women were still trying to establish themselves as professionals, and when they see a female attorney who seems to be causing women to lose ground, it makes them angry. When we showed them pictures of female attorneys and asked them to pick the most competent, they chose women wearing suits. The older the judge, the more conservative her taste. The exceptions were fashionable female judges who give women preferential treatment if they mirror their style. Most of them can be found in smaller jurisdictions, and they, like their male counterparts, are members of the local aristocracy.

Sometimes it is difficult to identify a judge's professional style. A number of judges said they dress less formally since becoming a judge, because the robe hides many flaws. It is obvious that they expect the women who appear before them to dress more formally than they do. What you have to find out is how the judge dressed when she was an attorney.

In most cases an attorney's style is personal; however, several female attorneys said the only time they changed their look was when they appeared before a feminist judge with a political agenda. They said that these judges favored those who look as if they hold the same beliefs they do. These judges are found almost exclusively in and around large metropolitan areas.

Dessing for the Jury

The reaction of juries to lawyers has been turned on its head, probably by the popularity of Court TV and the spate of high-profile celebrity cases.

The final survey I conducted before writing this book contradicted much of the past research; therefore I designed a new survey for this section.

With the cooperation of my client law firms I made up nine sets of videos and showed them to potential jurors in seven areas. In each set an attorney made the same argument wearing a conservative suit, a conservative feminine suit, a brightly colored or fashionable suit, a traditional jacket-and-skirt outfit, a lively skirt-and-jacket outfit, a conservative dress-and-jacket outfit, a conservative dress, a feminine but not sexy dress, a skirt and blouse, and a nontraditional jacket over a dress. Because much of the clothing was owned by the women, there was a wide variety of colors and styles, and we did consider them when interpreting the results. We did not test short or tight skirts, revealing blouses, pants, or any other garment that men thought of as cute or sexy, because the results of a survey using stills showed that they sent very negative messages to most jurors.

Grand jury members responded best to women in conservative suits. They showed no preference for masculine or feminine colors or styles as long as the suit was conservative. They were most impressed by attorneys wearing white or light blue blouses. They responded to an understated, affluent, businesslike look.

These are the only juries composed of Establishment members, and they have the prejudices of people who make it up. They believe that people with money are more talented and honest than those without. When you appear before a grand jury, something about you should scream money. They are not turned off by dark traditional suits, but I would not advise wearing one. Usually at least one woman on this jury is a fashionable dresser and will not pay much attention to a woman who is not.

"Old money" juries are extinct, but upper-middle-class juries can still be found in affluent areas of suburbia. They respond best to a conservative, well-tailored look. With these juries you must pay attention to how the women on the jury are dressed. If they are well dressed, you must also be well dressed. If you dress poorly by their standards, they will perceive you as lower status.

Wear an expensive, feminine, traditional stylish suit or jacket outfit when dealing with this group. You must look like an executive or professional and someone who is sophisticated enough to fit into their lifestyle to gain their respect. When I asked three successful attorneys what they wear before such a jury on the first day, one said an expensive, stylishly conservative, custom-made, maroonish brown suit with a pale blue blouse. The other two said they would wear Jones of New York suits that were stylish yet conservative. All three were right on target. All these suits tested well, but the suit that tested best before comfortable suburbanites was a medium-range gray worn with a light blue blouse.

Most suburban juries have a mix of ethnic and income groups. You can count on only two things—they are predominantly white and they are mostly middle class. Minorities on these juries, while sensitive about racial matters, are every bit as conservative and solidly middle class as the whites. The only outfit to wear before them is a suit. You can and should change its color and style depending on who is on the jury and whether you wish to come across as a friend or expert. Dark blue and medium-range gray suits say "legal expert," while earth tones say "friendly."

I met a number of successful lawyers who disagree with this advice. They regularly wear jacket outfits and dresses before juries and win. You can wear these outfits if your appearance, demeanor, and style is authoritative. In fact, I recommend dresses for attorneys whose style is aggressive or abrasive. However, most women practicing law have a soft, feminine approach, and they need to wear suits before middle-class juries.

At one time middle-class juries reacted negatively to signs of style or wealth—expensive jewelry, designer scarves, and the like. They read these things as fashionable and nonserious. This is no longer true—you can dress stylishly as long as you do not overdo it. If you are dressing to impress other female attorneys, you are overdoing it.

Blue-collar whites respond best to female attorneys in traditional blue, gray, and beige suits. They expect lawyers to look like lawyers, and older members of their group will not give much credence to a lawyer who does not look like a professional. They were turned off by women in light blue, maroon, and green suits and all but the most conservative and traditional jacket outfits. A gray skirt and a white blouse worn with a navy jacket worked best.

Urban juries, which are often composed of blue-collar whites and minorities, are a challenge. While the whites respond favorably to an Establishment look, blacks respond with distrust to that look. You can keep your credibility with blue-collar whites as long as you wear a traditional suit. It cannot be too traditional because blacks respond best to white female lawyers who wear earth tones. We found that brown tweed, herringbone, and plaid suits and jackets worked best for both groups. However, if there are more than two blacks on a jury, or they indicate through their dress or in any other way that they are anti-Establishment, wear a tweed jacket over a plain dress. There is only one look that turns off lower-income minorities more quickly than an Establishment look—and that is a dated Establishment look. Looking up-to-date helps.

Rural juries have changed. They now respond to the same kind of lawyers that the rest of us do. If you dress down, some of them will be offended.

Chapter Six

Color Me Successful

Before I speak to a group I try to find out as much about its members as possible. When I can, I arrive early so that I can look over the audience before my presentation. When I speak at a convention with an exhibit hall, I visit that as well because it sometimes gives me insight into the industry or group.

Several years ago a uniform company brought me in to speak at a law enforcement convention about designing police uniforms based on research. Before the speech I visited the company's exhibit hall and found many of the exhibits informative and entertaining. One company demonstrated robots that handled bombs, and another demonstrated bulletproof vests—a lot of fun for someone who loves shoot-'em-up movies.

However, the exhibit that stopped me dead in my tracks had a videotape showing how out-of-control prisoners calmed down when they were put in a pink room. The demonstrator started the presentation by explaining that an English company had conducted a series of studies that proved violent prisoners would calm down and be easier to handle if they were placed in a room painted a *specific* shade of pink. Then we were shown the video, which showed a large, extremely violent man being manhandled into a cell by a half dozen police officers. After being put in the cell, the man continued verbally to abuse police officers and tried to tear the cell apart. After ten minutes the police officers came in and restrained him once again. Once they had, they took him from that cell, down the hallway, and into another cell that was painted bright pink. Within ten minutes the man had calmed down. At this point a lone officer entered the second cell, removed the prisoner's restraints, and left him. The prisoner continued to sit on a cot calmly and quietly. He was no longer acting out violently.

The presenter then said, "Don't go away. I have something to show you that is equally important." He turned on the video again, and a second large, violent man was shown being forced into a cell by a phalanx of officers. This time the prisoner was placed in a bright pink cell that seemed to be identical to the previous pink-colored cell. But he did not calm down. In fact, he became even more violent. He not only began to rip the cell apart, he started ripping off his clothing. At that point the officers restrained him and took him across the hall to another pink cell. Within ten minutes he was sitting calmly and quietly, passively obeying the orders being given by the officers. The presenter asked how many of us had realized when we saw the pink cell that it was different from the one we had seen in the first video. Almost all of us admitted we hadn't noticed the difference. In fact, it was only after the presenter explained to us that the first cell in the second video was two shades lighter than the other pink cell that I thought I noticed the difference. Frankly, the difference was so subtle that it never occurred to me. But the prisoners, on a subconscious level, recognized the difference and reacted to it.

This is significant because our research shows similar reactions to subtle differences in shades of color in garments. Often a subtle difference in the shade of color of a garment will dramatically change its socioeconomic message. When we made the shade of yellow in a suit a bit harsher, it stopped sending the message that the wearer was upper middle class, sophisticated, and powerful and started sending the message that the wearer was lower class, unsophisticated, and without power.

We dressed a number of women in dresses, suits, and blouses that were identical in every way except for color and sent them into a variety of situations. We discovered that the colors and shades of color worn had an enormous impact on how people treated them. Very subtle changes in shades of color did affect the subjects' authority, status, credibility, and popularity. The obvious fact that different colors and different shades of color are flattering on some people and unflattering on others was not as important as a number of other variables.

I do not think that the "color me beautiful" and similar theories are valid—especially for women who want to build a successful working wardrobe. The idea that people and colors can be divided into four color groups—fall, winter, spring, and summer—flies in the face of common sense, experience, and research. These theories are based on three invalid assumptions. First, colors are divided into two groups, those with blue undertones, winter and summer, and those with yellow undertones, spring and fall. Second, colors are further divided into clear, winter and spring, and unclear, summer and fall. Any beginning art student will tell you that there are colors that do not fit neatly into any of these categories. Third, the secret to looking attractive is limiting your colors to the categories that match your skin tone. They overlook the obvious fact that beauty is in conditioning, if not in the eye of the beholder.

Even if the theories were valid, it would take a very talented artist to place most people in the right category. I have been on a number of TV shows with color consultants, and in the same year different "experts" told me that I was a spring, a winter, and a fall. I don't know why I didn't get summer, but I met one talk-show host who told me he was put into all four seasons by different color consultants.

The season you belong to is often a matter of personal opinion. Also, the colors that look good on you depend on when people see you. If you catch me on one of those rare occasions when I have a tan, the colors that will flatter me will be different from those that flatter me when I am my normal ghostly pale. For example, I have gray hair, and gray suits tend to be flattering. However, there is one shade of light gray that has just the opposite effect. That shade exactly picks up my hair, and for reasons I cannot explain the look is tacky.

Dividing each season into forty or fifty colors simply doesn't give a person enough options, because there are forty or fifty shades in each one of those colors, and any two shades may elicit a totally different reaction.

However, the greatest flaw in the "color me beautiful" theory is the assumption that if you put the right colors on a blue-eyed blonde or an olive-skinned brunette, they will be equally attractive to everyone. Research teaches us that is not so. We are all conditioned by our environment, and as a result people living in the Northeast see colors differently from people in California. In fact, in different cultures colors differ. When you ask the Chinese to identify red, not surprisingly most describe what we call "Chinese red." While most Americans see a shade closer to fire-engine red, Europeans, on the other hand, see a red that is not only lighter but tends toward orange. If you show a woman in a navy blue dress to a cross section of the

American public and ask them if that dress is attractive on her, you will find that you will get a far more positive response from people in New York, Boston, and other northern cities than you will from people in the Sun Belt. Conversely, if you show the same woman in a light blue dress, people in the Sun Belt are much more likely to think that dress flatters her than are people in northern cities.

After spending a small fortune trying to identify the best way of choosing colors that are flattering, I came to the conclusion that the method women have been using for years works best. When deciding on a garment, most women hold it in front of them and look in a mirror. The only way to really judge whether a color in a garment is right for you is to hold it against your skin. If you do not have the confidence or the taste to buy clothing this way, I suggest that you revert to the second most common method used by women when they shop. Take a friend with you and ask her advice. This is a case where the old tried-and-true methods work best.

The women I have questioned have told me loud and clear that they want to be as attractive as possible. However, if you think of looking attractive as your only goal when you are dressing for work, you are making a serious mistake. You must think in terms of being effective as well as attractive. They are not mutually exclusive, however; you have to keep both in mind when choosing colors. The colors and shades of color that help convince people that you are attractive also announce your status, effectiveness, attitude, loyalty, honesty, and credibility.

The first thing that any businesswoman should consider before choosing the color of a garment is the status message that color sends. Every woman understands that if she buys two garments, one in a very expensive store and one in an inexpensive store, she will not get garments with matching colors. In most cases it is easy to tell the difference between an expensive and inexpensive garment, even if the cut, design, and detailing seem identical. The most obvious difference is the fabric, which takes to dyes differently. In the better stores, colors generally have a soft, subtle look about them, while in the inexpensive stores they often have a harsh or electric quality.

The shade of color affects how people see the garment. When we showed garments in rich, upper-middle-class colors to a cross section of businesspeople, 73 percent thought that the garments were rich and well made. However, when we showed garments identical in every way except their colors, they were not perceived as subtle or rich looking by the same people. They described the garments as shabby and second-rate. If you wear the rich-looking garments, people will think you are first-class, on top of your job, and clever. If you wear garments with a harsh or electric look, people will think you are second-rate.

I have proven this over and over. While researching this book, I tested outfits purchased in different stores at a college job fair. I sent two young women with virtually identical résumés to meet with twenty-five recruiters. They were wearing black skirts, white blouses, and red jackets. The blouses and skirts were bought at a moderate-priced store. The jackets, although similar in appearance, were of different quality. One was purchased in a fine Fifth Avenue store in Manhattan, and the other was purchased at a discount house. The jackets looked so similar that one of the young women asked why I was wasting my time testing them; she was sure that nobody would notice the difference. After twelve visits the young women switched jackets so their personal styles would not affect the experiment.

The first young woman, when wearing the expensive red

jacket, received one job offer and three callbacks. The second woman, wearing the inexpensive jacket, received one callback. In the second round the young woman wearing the better jacket received a job offer and four callbacks, while the student wearing the inexpensive jacket struck out twelve times.

When we interviewed the young women, and psychology students who accompanied them, they agreed that when they were wearing the expensive jacket, they received preferential treatment. When wearing the better jacket, they were twice as likely to be asked to sit down and be told about the company. When wearing the cheaper jacket, the recruiters were more abrupt, and in one case, rude. There was a marked difference in the way these professional interviewers reacted to them. In addition, the psychology students who accompanied them noticed that the reaction was immediate. In three separate booths, the minute the interviewers saw the women, they changed their body language. When the applicant wore the expensive jacket, the recruiters' body language was more welcome and open. When they wore the inexpensive one, their body language was stiff and closed. There is no question that wearing upper-middle-class colors can make the difference between being accepted and rejected in the competitive job market.

We conducted a number of similar experiments with saleswomen who were selling to both female and male executives. We found that putting saleswomen in upper-middle-class colors increased their sales. In addition, saleswomen wearing upper-middle-class colors spent more time in clients' offices. Apparently clients were more willing to spend time with saleswomen when they looked affluent and successful. When they wore lower-class colors, the same saleswomen were treated shabbily. On several occasions the interview was ended by the buyer before the saleswoman could finish her presentation.

The saleswomen received good responses from two purchasing agents when wearing lower-middle-class colors. Interestingly, in both cases the buyer came from a blue-collar background. They were the exceptions, not the rule. Most people, no matter what their background, saluted when the young women came in wearing stylish upper-class colors, and the same women buyers put their noses up when they wore blue-collar colors.

If you cannot recognize the difference between upper-middle-class colors and lower-class colors, all you have to do is cross-shop. Work on one color per day. First, visit the best store in town and look at their medium blue coats, suits, blouses, scarves, and so on. Then visit an inexpensive store and look at the same garments. The differences in the shades of color should be obvious. Next time, repeat the exercise with another color. After about thirty visits, most of the women who have tried this method have no problems picking colors.

What makes this ability so important is that the class message sent by color apparently affects a woman's chances of becoming an executive or manager. When we studied women in executive positions in seven companies we found they wore only upper-middle-class colors. Apparently the glass ceiling is harder to penetrate while wearing lower-class colors. The women who move into the top ranks in American corporations almost invariably come from upper-middle-class backgrounds or have upper-middle-class taste and wear upper-middle-class colors, while those who look, act, or sound as though they come from less sophisticated backgrounds—no matter how talented—never make it into the executive suites. The glass ceiling is in many cases a *class* ceiling. There is no question that in business class carries clout.

A number of years ago a psychologist was hired by the New

York City Police Department to redesign the uniform in hopes of cutting down the number of assaults on police officers. When he undertook the job, the police officers in New York were wearing dark navy pants and a dark navy shirt. He concluded that the officers were assaulted by people who were terrified when approached by the police. Since people who are frightened were most likely to strike out, he decided to make the uniform less threatening. He changed the shirt from a navy to a medium blue.

Two things happened immediately. First, the number of assaults on police officers went down dramatically and stayed down, and second, many of the officers were unhappy about the change. They reported that the minute they put on the lighter-colored shirt, they didn't command the respect they had in the past. Several traffic officers requested the darker shirt because of their precarious posts. They said that when they were wearing the navy shirt and they put up their hand, signaling pedestrians to stop, everybody stopped. The minute they put on the lighter blue shirt, fewer people stopped. Some even walked right past them as if they were not there, and this made their job more difficult. I have no doubt that if they reissued dark shirts, the traffic cops would have commanded more respect.

If you have problems with authority, giving orders, or commanding the respect of people working for you or with you, wearing darker colors will help. If co-workers or clients regularly question your professional competence, you probably could use more authority in your wardrobe. If you wear light-colored dresses, jackets, or suits to work, stop. If you wear the same garments in darker colors, you will be more effective.

However, if you are very large, or have a gruff or very aggressive style, you would be wise to avoid very dark garments. If you intimidate people, dark colors may only make your problem worse. You would be wise to soften your colors and your look.

There are rules for choosing colors. First, you always must stick within the natural range of colors worn by people in your position. If everyone in your position wears khaki pants and navy T-shirts, you must wear them as well. You cannot separate yourself from those in your group or you will alienate them. However, there are very few offices where everybody wears identical outfits. In most offices a wide variety of garments is worn by both men and women.

If you work in a conservative environment and would like to have more influence with men, particularly those born before 1947, wear traditional male business colors: navy, medium blue, dark, medium, and light gray, and beige with a touch of gray in it. However, if dressing conservatively would separate you from your fellow co-workers, you can still increase your visual authority by choosing outfits that are just a bit darker and just a bit more conservative than your co-workers. If you are not comfortable dressing this way every day, it will help if you dress in darker garments on those occasions when you need people to listen to you or follow your lead or when you are likely to have your authority or professional competence challenged.

The fashion people have decided that red is a powerful color. There is no doubt that many of the most successful and powerful women in the country wear red jackets. Red is a sexual color, and women who feel powerful wearing red do so for the traditional reason—they can attract a man's attention and get him to do what they want him to do. It certainly is a type of power, but it is not the type of power that works in most business settings.

If you are looking for power and authority, stay away from vibrant colors and stick to darker ones. Forget the description of the so-called power garments recommended by fashion people: they are really talking about sexual power.

Finally, if you wish to be taken seriously and be authoritative, you must remember that men and women look at clothing differently. If you saw a man in a pink suit, you would think that he was crazy, tasteless, or color blind. However, most women think a woman wearing a traditionally tailored pink suit is dressed appropriately for business. But unless she works in a totally female environment, she is not. Men react to colors differently. Over the years they have been conditioned to think of people wearing traditional business colors as being effective. When dealing with men, particularly if you wish them to take your advice on important matters, wearing traditional male colors in your primary garment will give you an advantage.

The first experiments I conducted showing the impact of color were originally designed only to see if women in management could break the dress for success rules and succeed. I worked with groups of fifty women in New York, Chicago, Detroit, and Boston. Each of these women was identified by their companies as an effective and efficient manager or executive. I had each of them keep a clothing calendar. In the morning they recorded what they were wearing to work, and at the end of the day they answered a series of questions. The questions varied from woman to woman, profession to profession, and company to company, but all were asked how they were treated by their subordinates, co-workers, and superiors and whether anyone questioned their professional competence.

To our shock and surprise, we found out that these women faced over 50 percent of the challenges to their authority or competence between June 28 and Labor Day. When I went back and looked carefully at these calendars, I found that these women invariably had most of their challenges on days when they wore light colors. The color of the garments these women wore was only one factor affecting the way they were treated, but it was a critical one. Simply by changing the color of the garments they wore, we changed the way they were treated. This survey showed that traditional male colors worked best for most women in authority positions.

This research was in 1972, and things have changed. In the early 1970s women were more likely to challenge other women when they dressed in soft, feminine colors. Today that is no longer true. Women have convinced themselves that feminine colors are effective. The problem is that they haven't convinced men. If you work with men and you wear soft pastels, it is almost an invitation to be challenged by one-third of the men.

My first clients were law firms. I researched the most effective clothing for male attorneys in the early 1960s. That was a time when the stringent dress codes of the 1950s were beginning to break down, and a number of the older attorneys were upset by the way some of the younger attorneys were dressing. When women started joining these law firms in large numbers in the seventies and eighties, these firms hired me to research their clothing as well. I discovered most shades of green, lavender, and gold, plus any color or shade of color that was unique or different, made female attorneys less credible with judges and juries. We also found that if a female attorney wore unique color combinations, even if they were aesthetically pleasing, judges and juries questioned her credibility.

Wearing anything new or unusual will make it difficult to get people, particularly strangers, to trust you. This does not mean you can wear a shade of color that was introduced last month or six months ago. Most men will describe a new shade of color as strange or unusual a year after it has been introduced and are less likely to believe a woman wearing that color. Anything that upsets the norm hurts credibility, and fashion colors upset the norm. You can wear fashion colors only if they are retrofashions or when the newest color is not new at all.

I do not wish to create the impression that color only creates problems. The fact is, using color correctly can give businesswomen an advantage over men. Because women wear a great many colors, they can use color to solve problems. The first and most obvious problem that color can solve is not being noticed. You can wear a very bright color that by its nature draws attention to you, or you can wear sharp contrasts, which has the same effect. If you wear a bright yellow or red dress or jacket, you will get noticed. This is one of the reasons I believe bright red jackets are so popular with women. It enhances their sense of presence, people notice them, and this can be very important.

One problem faced by women is that they are overlooked. Most women believe that since men generally run meetings, they favor other men. When we researched this problem we found that sexism was only one factor. When we studied the videotapes of nineteen meetings, attended by an equal number of men and women of equal rank and ability, we found that men tended to dominate the meetings. The person in charge, whether male or female, called on men more often. In those meetings where there was no formal procedure for calling on someone, the person running the meeting tended to direct his or her attention to men. They also tended to weigh the ideas of men more heavily. We taped several meetings where a woman put forth an idea that was ignored, but a few minutes later, when a man put forth the same idea, it was taken seriously.

Ironically, when we went back and looked at these tapes, a number of the women who were doing the complaining were as guilty of the sin of antifeminine sexism as any man.

When we measured the number of times women interrupted women and men, we found women interrupted other women 54 percent more often than men. It wasn't something they did consciously; it was a matter of habit. Two women often talk at once without insulting each other. If a man is interrupted, he takes umbrage, and probably as a result, both men and women are less likely to interrupt a man when he is speaking. We also saw that men were more likely to speak out and stand up without being called on. They were more likely to put forth an opinion on most subjects. We also noticed that when a man and a woman started talking at the same time, in seven out of ten cases the woman backed off and the man kept talking. At first we thought that it was male verbal patterns and aggressiveness that caused them to dominate meetings in which they had no more to contribute than the women, but a second experiment proved that this was only part of the reason.

I have run a sales training company for years and have been doing sales research for almost twenty years, and one of the things I discovered early on is that people buy from people they like. At first I thought that was the nature of things: some people were born popular and others weren't. However, after close examination it became evident that being popular was nothing more than sending the right verbal and nonverbal signals, and it is a teachable skill. In fact, I researched my book on popularity at the same time that I researched and wrote this book for women. Today I speak on popularity more often than I do on clothing.

One of the projects we conducted for the popularity research was to videotape social gatherings. We focused on groups of people who worked together. Our original intent was to see if popular people were more likely to be listened to when they spoke. They were. However, when we took a second look at the tapes, we discovered that physically large people dominated most groups. The biggest men almost invariably dominated the direction of the group, even when they only spoke up occasionally. They commanded more respect than shorter men and women, and their ideas were weighed more heavily. Although most of the time big men dominate groups, when a large woman is part of the group she is as likely to dominate the group as a tall man.

Since being big gives one a sense of presence and authority, I tested developing a sense of presence using color. We took six women at a convention who were wearing subdued colored blouses and gave them red blouses. We asked them to change into the red blouses about halfway through the cocktail party. We did not tell them why we wanted them to change. The minute they changed, they became more effective in groups. In subsequent testing we discovered that the best garment to wear to such a gathering was a bright red jacket.

An electrical engineer named Jackie found that wearing at least one eye-catching item changed the way her fellow engineers treated her. She worked as an in-house consultant with seven other computer specialists. When they were faced with a major undertaking, they followed a standard procedure. After one or more of them studied the problem, the group would gather and plan a solution. In these planning sessions they would decide what had to be done, who should undertake the project, and, if more than one person was needed, who would be in charge. Jackie felt that her suggestions were often overlooked and she hardly ever was put in charge, in spite of the fact that she thought she was one of three qualified to run a team. The group consisted of six men, all of whom were five feet ten or taller and one woman who was five feet nine. Jackie was five feet one and weighed 103 pounds.

The first time she wore a bright red jacket to a planning session she said that she felt she had more power. Three days later when they called the next meeting, she was wearing a navy suit with a white blouse, so she tied a bright red scarf at her neck and replaced her belt with another one. She said she did not look great, but she was sure she would be noticed. That day for the first time they bought her solution and put her in charge of a project that had originally been given to someone else. She now keeps a collection of bright scarves and eye-catching jewelry in her desk just for such occasions.

It is important that women understand, if you meet a woman who is five feet nine, she may think of herself as big, but in a man's world she is not. If she is working with five men whose average height is five feet ten, she is small, because most women's bodies and faces are slighter. Wearing a brightly colored garment or eye-catching jewelry that draws attention to her will act as a leveler.

Through trial and error we came up with a number of techniques for using color to create a sense of presence in conservative business environments. Bright red jackets are fine, but you cannot wear one every day. If you work with men and women who usually wear blue and gray suits, a bright red jacket may separate you visually from the group and make you less effective. A woman would be better off wearing a dark suit with a maroon, red, or yellow blouse or accentuating her outfit with a bright scarf or a strong piece of jewelry worn at her neck. Contrast can sometimes be strong enough to draw attention to a person. For example, a woman wearing a navy suit and a dark blouse accentuated with a white silk scarf would certainly be noticed. The women who handle this problem most effectively are those who have panache and use accessories well. The minute they understood the principle, they applied it beautifully.

Colors, in addition to drawing attention to the wearer, can mark a person either as an outsider or a team player. It is a simple statistical fact that women who work in male-dominated fields are more likely to succeed if they adopt a feminine version of the male dress code.

We asked men who worked in twenty male-dominated industries to describe the women with whom they worked. Women whose main garments were usually in male colors, including those found in male sportswear, were 79 percent more likely to be described as serious about their careers than women who regularly wore feminine colors.

One of the most interesting experiments ever conducted on the effect of wearing different colors was the red and blue hat experiment. A psychologist picked people at random and sent them into a room to perform simple tasks: pick up chairs, fold papers, and stuff envelopes. The nature of the tasks was such that they could perform them anywhere in the room. This gave those participating the freedom to associate with any other person in the room. As they entered, the psychologist randomly assigned each person a blue or a red hat. When the psychologist returned an hour later, he found that all the people wearing blue hats were working in one section of the room, while all the people with red hats were working in the other. He called them out individually and asked them why they were working apart. The answer from both groups was the same. They said they didn't have anything against the people wearing the other color hats, but somehow they didn't feel comfortable with them or trust them. They felt more comfortable with people wearing hats the same color as theirs.

We conducted experiments on company dress codes and found that the clothing people wore had an impact on how they got along in the office. We discovered that people who dressed in a different style or in different colors from their co-workers generally didn't get along as well as those who fit in visually.

Jilly, an accountant on the West Coast, was laid off several years ago. She asked her best friend to find out why she was let go while others who were not as effective as she was were not. Jilly was outraged when her friend said the boss thought she was not a team player. She said she always cooperated with the other people in the office—in fact, several of the accountants who were still working at the company created problems she smoothed over.

When she started with a new company several months later they sent her for a video consultation. When I saw her video I did not know about her previous job but took one look and told her she was wearing the wrong colors. She objected vehemently. She said she was an "autumn," and most of the colors she could wear were earth tones. After debunking the color analysis based on seasons, I pointed out that accounting is a conservative blue-and-gray business. I said if 90 percent of her business clothing was in earth tones, it would create the impression that she was not a team player and could cause problems for her. When she heard that, she agreed to change her working wardrobe and told me about her previous job.

After she had been with the company for over two years I asked her how she was getting along. She said she was very happy; in her last review her manager wrote that her attitude made her a great asset to the team.

Colors, of course, can be used to disassociate you from people and ideas. A client of mine became president of a very large company. The company had several disastrous years, and it was his job to rebuild it. His plan for recovery required the company's profit margins to shrink. He had to invest in the company's manufacturing facilities and development of new products. At the end of a year and a half he told me that he had a real problem. He didn't think he was going to keep his job. At the first stockholders' meeting, they almost voted him out. It never got to that, but he was worried about the next stockholders' meeting. They hated to see their profits drop, even though as a group they understood there was no choice if they wanted to see the company ultimately prosper. He asked me to look at videos of the meeting and see if I could help him manage the next meeting more successfully.

It was obvious that he had made a couple of mistakes. The speakers covered two topics, the first explaining why profits were so low and the second outlining the progress in research and new product development. Unfortunately my client thought that it was his duty as president to deliver the bad news, so he got up and told the stockholders that the company had lost money and it was going to continue to lose money over the next year. Then he went on to describe the company's bright future.

When I spoke to him about it, he said that it would be impossible for him just to get up and give the good news and let someone else give the bad news. He was convinced it would not work and would only exacerbate the situation.

Nevertheless he took my suggestions. The next year he had a vice president in charge of bad news get up and describe the financial condition of the company. Following Mr. Bad News, he had another vice president get up and describe the rosy future of the company. After the good news vice president finished, the president spoke, summarizing what Mr. Bad News said quickly, honestly, and frankly, but the message had less of an impact because they had heard it all before. The president went on to expand on what Mr. Good News had said. In addition, Mr. Bad News wore a dark gray suit, a white shirt, and blue tie. Mr. Good News wore a medium-range blue suit, a white shirt, and maroon tie. My friend wore an outfit that was very similar to the one worn by the good news vice president.

We surveyed the audience after the meeting. Most of the people we questioned associated the president with the good news, mainly because he was associated visually with the man who had first delivered the good news.

Since then I have arranged to package a number of presidents and chairmen of the board of companies for stockholder meetings. We have always used a principle of "color association."

There is an even more sophisticated use of color. I wrote a column several years back discussing a problem common among women managers—how to handle reprimanding employees. To get their point across, the female managers sometimes went too far and seemed to lose control by yelling and shouting, while male managers were able to scare the blazes out of people without screaming or yelling. (This is not to say that male managers don't scream and yell.) When the female managers in one company read my column they were annoyed, but they agreed it was probably true. One woman wrote to tell me how the managers decided to solve the problem: each was going to buy a black suit and wear it only when she was going to reprimand someone. Black suits in that company became known as the "kick me" suits. The minute they heard that, they said, they knew the black suits were working.

Once they started using black suits, the word spread rapidly throughout the company. Everyone knew when a manager wore a black suit someone was in trouble. The managers said that when their people saw them wearing a black suit, they were intimidated.

I was so intrigued by the woman's letter, I arranged to visit her office. When she returned from lunch that afternoon wearing her black suit, I could see how effective it was. The first thing I noticed was the reaction of her subordinates, who had been friendly and chatting with her as we left for lunch but did not look at or speak to her afterward.

By the way, a few years later, on my advice, she and her fellow managers dropped the black suit. They had established their authority. The "kick me" suits were no longer necessary.

Several years later I was hired to package an anchorwoman in one of the smaller markets on the East Coast. Her boss told me that she had a unique problem. The audience loved her, but they didn't take her seriously. When asked to describe her, most said she was nice but not serious or knowledgeable. In fact, she had two master's degrees from an Ivy League school and was very knowledgeable.

When I looked at her wardrobe, I understood why she was not taken seriously. She dressed almost exclusively in "like me" colors: yellow, beige, and blue. She was very attractive, and people loved her. My solution was to get her three blazers in "respect me" colors—a medium blue, a medium-dark gray, and a midnight navy. She wore those jackets on evenings when the news was serious but kept the midnight blue for very heavy stories.

The reaction of the audience was very interesting. After three months she was taken more seriously, and after six months she had tremendous impact when delivering a serious story. A number of listeners said they didn't know why, but they knew something terrible had happened the minute they saw her on screen. The dark navy jacket telegraphed the fact that she was serious, and it made her more effective.

Only women can wear earth tones and look effective and professional. That may not seem like a tremendous advantage, but it is. If you are in the business of counseling people on personal matters or getting people to like and trust you, wearing earth tones will make your job easier. There is no question that wearing earth tones will make you more effective, more trustworthy, and more likable. Ministers giving advice to parishioners, psychologists dealing with patients, and lawyers approaching juries are more effective in earth tones.

The garment that tested best was a medium-range brown tweed jacket with beige or orange accent threads. Earth-tone outfits calm people down, reassure them that you like them, and are nonthreatening. They are the garments for the charmers. In summer and spring you can add pale yellow to earth tones and you will look friendly. Pale yellow says "I'm a nice person, I'm easygoing, I'm likable, I like you, and I'm not threatening."

If you remember only one thing from this chapter, remember this: Sometimes bright colors draw attention to you. Sometimes dark colors make you an authority figure. Sometimes upper-class colors give you dignity and power, but earth tones win people over, and if you choose carefully, they will allow you to fit in and look effective in almost any setting. If you remember nothing else, remember that.

If you have built your wardrobe around seasonal colors, you have been unnecessarily limiting your wardrobe choices and in some cases forcing yourself into colors that are not flattering. You should immediately start testing the items you purchased the old-fashioned way. Hold them up against your body and take independent judgments. If you are convinced that you have made all the right choices, ask a friend whose taste you respect to validate them.

Using video consultations, I have freed many women from the limited color trap.

Mary was lucky. She worked in a conservative company and was told she was a "winter." She was a stunning brunette with brown eyes and a light olive complexion. She was of Italian extraction, married to an Irishman. She told me she had been darker but now rarely goes out in the sun, so her color had lightened. Her wardrobe was dominated by navy, gray, and black in suits, jackets, and dresses. The other colors that were important in her business wardrobe were red, medium blue, and burgundy. Her choices worked, with the exception of a purple dress and bright pink blouse, which I advised her to save for weekends. Mary's color consultant had also recommended an electric yellow blouse that screamed "blue collar." I told her to throw it out and not to give it to the Salvation Army because it would not be a nice thing to do to a poor person. She showed me a pale gray blouse that she'd bought because it was among her recommended colors, but it made her look sickly. She didn't like and couldn't wear most of the recommended colors in blouses. She wore mainly white blouses and complained that the winter blouse colors—pale green, gray, red, and turquoise—were either very conservative or wild. She wanted a few outfits that would make it easier for her to get people to cooperate with her.

For blouses, I recommended pale yellow, pale blue, a slightly darker blue, and very pale pink; and for suits, beige, medium blue, and light gray. I suggested she purchase her suits and blouses at the same time so she could see the entire look, and start by putting the soft yellow and pale pink blouses with her navy and gray suits. I wanted to soften Mary's image because she was having difficulty eliciting the cooperation of her fellow workers. I recommended that on days when she needed others to go along with her, she wear the slightly darker blue with her new beige suit. It is a traditional, soft look and very effective with men. Finally I advised Mary to stop rejecting garments just because they were not on her list.

On the follow-up consultation a year later Mary reported that she had expanded far beyond my selections. She'd read a column I wrote on earth tones and bought a rich brown suit that she wears with a blue or pale yellow blouse. Since she'd expanded and softened her image she was given customer contact assignments, which was the next step up for Mary. Her boss told her she'd received the assignment because she was much friendlier—and he let only friendly people deal with clients.

Amy, twenty-six, a new manager in a telephone company, was told she was a "summer." She is five feet tall and weighs about one hundred pounds. She has fair skin, blue eyes, and a ruddy complexion. She owned one suit and two jackets. She described the suit as "gray navy." It was a medium gray and light blue combination. With it she wore white, light blue, rose, and pink blouses. Her jackets were red and dark green. She had nine dresses she wore to work. Half of them came from color analysis cards that a color consultant had given her to use when she shopped. She liked the cards, but they also frustrated her because she said she could hardly ever match them and was never sure when she had a match because the colors on the paper had a different quality from the colors on fabric.

When I asked her what she wanted her clothing to do, she said, "Make it easier for me to give orders." She was the assistant department head in a department where most of the women were in their forties, and some objected to taking orders from a "kid" who looked twenty-one. I started by telling her not to wear her bright red, pale pink, or pale purple dresses or her periwinkle blouse to work. I suggested that she purchase a navy suit. When she objected, I put off her consultation until that afternoon. I instructed her to purchase a navy suit in a local store but not to take off the tags or have it altered. That afternoon I had her put on the jacket and showed her that it was not only authoritative, but flattering. I told her she could stick with the blouses recommended—pale yellow, paler pink, light and off white—but most of her main garments would have to be darker than the ones she had if she wanted to give effective orders. When she complained that she could not find the shades of color recommended for suits, I told her she could wear medium blue, medium gray, and dark gray. I explained that she could not wait until the suit manufacturers came out with the exact shades that flattered her; she had to look like an executive now. I also explained that she could look attractive and effective if she threw away those cards and trusted her taste.

Six months later she wrote and thanked me. She said that after she started dressing more seriously, she had few difficulties with the older women. She believed that widening her choices made her dress with more style, not less. She sent me pictures, and I agreed.

Clara was a light-skinned African American lawyer whose entire wardrobe was in earth tones. Her suits were olive, brown, taupe, and tan, and her blouses were very light tan, golden beige, gold, and mustard. She had a sense of color and style, and she looked good. However, she worked for a brokerage house, and all the male and most of the female lawyers wore blue and gray. She performed a number of jobs, but her primary function was to negotiate for her firm.

In my opinion her color consultant hit the aesthetic bull's-eye—she chose colors that were very flattering. However, in order for Clara to succeed, she had to convince strangers that she was a competent professional. Most people, black and white, do not automatically think of black women as power figures. Clara needed, therefore, to wear power clothing to work. Her professional status demanded it. I recommended she wear traditional solid and pin-striped blue and gray suits with white blouses. She said she would give it a try. African Americans usually take my advice because they are very aware—often painfully aware—that how you look affects how people treat you.

I contacted Clara before writing about her. She said that after two months she changed her entire work wardrobe. There was no question that wearing traditional blue and gray suits helped her impress the people she needed to impress, and that was her primary goal. She said she went to law school to impress people not with her taste, but with her brains.

If you are told you are an "autumn" or "summer," your chances of success are far less than anyone who is told she is a "winter." Both seasons' selections are dominated by nonauthoritative colors, and since most women need all the authority they can get, most women who dress for these seasons are dressing for failure. Some women stay within the guidelines and still look like professionals, given plenty of time and money.

However, if you have been told you are a "spring" and you try to stay within the guidelines and choose mainly light vibrant colors, you are certainly dressing for failure. If you have been told you are a spring, you must disregard the advice and start from scratch.

If you hire a personal shopper or image consultant, you should ask her about her background. In about half the cases, when personal consultants dress people they dress them for failure. If you would not allow a personal consultant to edit your résumé, you probably should not let her choose your wardrobe.

Remember, the colors you wear announce your success, background, status, authority, personality, and more. Choose them carefully.

Chapter Seven

Looking Good

In twenty-two years, I estimate that I have answered about four thousand letters in my newspaper column. Ironically, the letter that created the biggest hubbub was one from a female attorney that I printed but didn't answer.

Three years before writing the letter, she had graduated from law school and gone to work for one of the top law firms in her hometown. A year and a half later she'd moved to another town and gone to work for a new firm. She explained that she'd left the first firm because nobody took her seriously. Apparently the partners could not get past the fact that she was strikingly beautiful.

Before switching cities and firms, she went to a top-notch makeup artist and asked him to make her look plain. When she liked what she saw, she had him instruct her on how to maintain that look. Her term for the process was "making-down." She didn't make herself unattractive—her object was not to look strikingly beautiful.

He styled her hair and applied makeup that made her look more drab. In less than a year and a half she had been given several important assignments and received two promotions and was considered one of the up-and-coming lawyers in her new firm.

I didn't agree or disagree with the letter. I thought it was such an interesting letter that I ran it in my column unanswered, and I told my readers that was the reason I was printing it.

Nevertheless I received an avalanche of letters, a majority of which condemned me for printing such a letter. Some said that I hated women, others said I was just plain stupid, and a few thought I was part of an antifeminist plot, while most only sneered at my lack of insight. In their minds, trying to tell women that looking beautiful isn't an advantage under all circumstances was silly.

Buried in this wave of criticism were also about a dozen letters from women who said that they had done exactly the same thing as the attorney who felt stymied by her beauty. Four women sent before and after pictures. Three of the four women were so beautiful that no matter what they did, they remained attractive, but they were no longer strikingly beautiful. Nine of the twelve reported that changing their appearance had a positive effect on the way they were treated at work. Six echoed the attorney—they were being treated as professionals for the first time. Most were well-educated, serious career women who felt that their beauty hindered their professional advancement. They took steps to rectify the problem and saw no reason to apologize. Six thanked me for printing the letter because they thought they were the only ones to "make-down."

There was no question that being feminine and alluring was not an asset when I did the original research in the early 1970s. That is why a woman dressed in a man-tailored skirted suit in traditional "male colors" that most women considered dull was thought of as effective by most men. For the same reason, I recommended wearing little or no makeup, doing without nail polish, and not wearing eyeshadow. At the time, anything that touched of feminine paint or powder announced to most businessmen that a woman was not a serious businessperson.

Around 1986 that began to change. Men started responding positively to women who wore feminine attire. Suits and jacket outfits in feminine colors, patterns, and styles started working as well as the "imitation male look."

By 1989–90 a more feminine approach by women in business was not only accepted, but often worked better than the masculine, serious approach that had worked several years before.

At the same time, my sales research had begun to uncover similar information. We found for the first time that a woman selling high-priced products was more successful when she used a nonsexy but feminine approach. Women who looked more austere or masculine were not as effective when selling to men. The change was so dramatic and important that I started running a sales course for women only.

It was at one of these training sessions that a young woman challenged me. She argued that if a feminine approach worked best, my advice on makeup and hairstyles should be updated. It was her contention that wearing her hair down over her shoulders made her much more attractive. She said she didn't look good with short hair, and since being feminine and attractive was now an asset, she thought she should wear her hair long. Our research on hair length told us she was wrong. However, whether she was right about the importance of being attractive was a question that I had never thoroughly researched, and she made me realize that it was a question I had to investigate.

Over the next year I reviewed the videotapes of women

selling both in traditional business and social settings. My staff and I divided the women on the tapes into five groups: very beautiful, attractive, above average, average, and below average. Most women were assigned to the same group by almost everybody, even though men and women have different concepts of feminine beauty. Some women are very sensual, and most men sense it immediately, while most women do not. Women also think thin is attractive, while most men like women with curves. Another difference is that women look at specifics about other women—the size of her nose, the shape of her legs, her hair color—while men generally look at the whole person.

When deciding which group to assign to the women, I weighed men's opinions equally with women's. I did, however, consider their different perspectives when doing the research. Any woman whom men and women rated very differently, I tested separately.

Once the women had been put into groups based on their physical appearance, we divided the women in each group according to how they dressed. Our objective was to test those who wore conservative dresses, chic dresses, sexy dresses, traditional suits, feminine suits, jacket outfits, and so forth only against other women similarly dressed. This eliminated clothing as a variable.

After we divided the women according to how they dressed, it became obvious that a woman's age and socioeconomic background affected the way businesspeople saw her. Eliminating age as a factor was easy. Since most of our executives were in their mid-thirties and early forties, we only tested them against women about the same age.

The influence of class created a more complex problem. While there were almost an equal number of executives and secretaries in the study, the executives questioned were three times as likely to identify upper-class women as attractive. Since executives are often upper middle class, obviously looking upper middle class was as important as or more important than physical beauty. Therefore we also tested the class message sent by cosmetics, hair, and other factors.

The first thing we discovered was that being attractive helps, but being beautiful does not. Very beautiful young women have difficulty being taken seriously, especially by men, most of whom refuse to even think of them as experts or authority figures. In addition, beautiful women are seen by both sexes as lacking in intelligence—or, at least, as lightweights. One reason they are seen in this light is that they have been traditionally portrayed in movies and on TV as dumb or shallow; if they have a thought in their heads, it is about how they look. This stereotype is obviously not true, but it is part of our culture, and it affects the way most people react to beautiful women.

Ironically, while being beautiful makes it very difficult for a woman to be taken seriously, being attractive makes it easier. Attractive women receive preferential treatment from most people, in and out of business. We sent attractive women to interview for positions ranging from secretary to vice president and found they were 20 percent more likely to be hired by women and almost three times more likely to be offered a job by men. We did not factor in the obvious advantage they had getting the interview in the first place. The men seemed anxious to spend time with them.

I ran two focus groups of attractive women. The women in both groups knew that their looks gave them an advantage, especially with men. However, a number of them complained that other women treated them poorly because they were jealous. Half of them said that they had been denied jobs or promotions because they believed the woman making the decision was jealous. (I don't know how valid their reasoning was, but I suspect there was some validity since so many of them voiced the same complaint.)

Nevertheless, any disadvantages that come as a result of being attractive do not even come close to offsetting the tremendous advantage that women get from being attractive. Research shows that they are hired quicker, promoted more often, and earn more money than less attractive women with similar qualifications. It is not surprising, because most of us, in spite of evidence to the contrary, assign positive attributes twice as often to attractive women. We believe they are more honest, clever, friendly, and easier to get along with than their less attractive sisters.

BECOMING MORE ATTRACTIVE

All this information would be interesting but useless if a woman could not make herself more attractive. So we researched what made a woman attractive, particularly to executives, and how becoming more attractive would affect her career. We discovered that the majority of businesswomen, once they learned to style their hair and use makeup effectively, could make themselves more attractive. We also discovered we could not give women a magic formula, but if we set them in the right direction and made a few suggestions, it helped. That is the object of this chapter.

While researching which women were considered attractive, I discovered there are different ways to be attractive. The healthy outdoor energetic look, the high-fashion look, the conservative chic look, the dainty feminine look, and the sexy look all can be very attractive. Looking good is an asset no matter how you achieve it, but most women are more attractive when they choose a style that suits them and their position.

The look that tested best among women under thirty-five was the healthy outdoor energetic look. The most attractive of these women could never be models in a Paris fashion show, but they might play the girl next door in a commercial. This look works particularly well for women with male bosses and those who deal with or work for large companies. It is also the ideal look for most saleswomen under thirty-five, including those selling themselves at job interviews.

Only about 10 percent of the women who were seen as excellent examples of this look come by it naturally—most work at it.

Julie, a civil engineer, was average looking and thought a high-fashion look made her more attractive. She wore fashionable outfits and applied her makeup like a *Vogue* model, with great care and considerable skill. She had a reputation as one of the best engineers in her department and had received several raises and one promotion. However, after seven years in the company she felt she was not being prepared for management. The other top engineers with her experience were being given more freedom and were getting premanagement field assignments, but she was not. When she questioned the managing engineer he did not give her a satisfactory answer as to why she had not received such assignments.

She signed up for a personal video consultation only because she wanted to learn to apply makeup more skillfully. When I told her I thought she chose the wrong style in makeup, she was insulted. She said she could prove I was wrong. She had just been assigned to a new office for a major project in the

Midwest. In less than two months she would be leaving, and she would change her style and keep one of my calendars. Since I had been hired to speak at the next corporate meeting, she planned to challenge me with her own research statistics.

When she stood up at the next meeting, I was expecting to be challenged. Instead Julie reported that when she changed her style, healthy outdoor energetic, attractive, the attitude of both her male and female supervisors changed as well. The men started treating her more like "one of the guys." She said they were rougher on her, but for the first time she felt like a full member of the team. The managing engineers assumed she could handle field assignments and gave them to her without her asking.

Nine months after Julie shortened her hair and started wearing understated makeup and less fashionable outfits, she was given her first management assignment. Everyone in the audience knew that if she succeeded with the first few management assignments, bigger jobs and more money would follow. After her speech we had to stay an extra day to handle the number of women who demanded personal consultations.

Mary Jane was a salesperson and spent two-thirds of her time on the road. An attractive twenty-six-year-old, she applied minimum makeup in minimum time and got away with it. Her look was acceptable by any standards. I suggested she put a little more effort into her image. After going to a class on how to apply makeup, she spent approximately five minutes, as she said, "putting on her new face" in the morning. She believed it helped her sales because she looked more attractive and found it easier to get appointments with men.

The high-fashion look does not work in most companies, but if you work for a fashionable woman, you must mirror her style. Women who spend time, effort, and money to look as though they stepped out of *Vogue* believe, like some people who exercise, that they are superior beings and respect only other women who do likewise.

Ellen, who had worked as a tax specialist for a Big Eight accounting firm, moved to a small town in the South when her husband inherited the family business. The only firm in town that could use her services had just one woman as a partner. This woman, to whom she reported, traveled to New York, Dallas, and Atlanta to buy her clothes. She always looked as if she walked out of a Fifth Avenue Manhattan boutique. Ellen tried to dress up her conservative look, but it did not work. Finally, out of desperation, she bought three fashionable suits and changed her hairstyle and makeup. The minute she changed, the female partner accepted her as an equal and a friend. Two years later she campaigned for Ellen to be made a partner. Today Ellen dresses conservatively when she deals with big clients but changes her look on those days when she knows she will be dealing with the senior partner.

There are, of course, a number of high-fashion looks. When we showed pictures of attractive, fashionable women to both businessmen and -women, the high-fashion look that garnered the best responses could best be described as elegant. "Fashionably elegant" even worked on Wall Street. If you are a fashionable dresser, keep in mind that trendy, innovative, eye-catching, and exotic never work with male executives.

"Conservative chic" is the style chosen by the most successful women. When I asked the women in my phone tag group why most of them chose this look at least part of the time, they said that it was the look most successful men responded to best. The ten pictures these women chose as examples of conservative chic were very similar. Only one woman wore a traditional dress for success suit with a white blouse and pumps. What made the look chic was the fact that the suit was obviously expensive, beautiful-ly tailored, and worn with an expensive gold necklace, a Rolex watch, a designer attaché, and other status items. Two wore very stylish suits in traditional menswear colors with obviously expensive accessories. Three were women in expensive stylish feminine suits, and two were wearing beautifully styled jackets: a red jacket over a black skirt and white blouse, and a navy one over a taupe dress. They chose only one woman in a dress without a jacket. It was a rich, conservative, tailored, navy, heavy wool model, worn by a forty-six-year-old woman with beautiful but tasteful jewelry. Its drape hid her figure, and it was as austere as any dress for success suit.

We have recommended this style for businesswomen because more successful women reported that their careers took off as soon as they switched to the conservative chic look than any other. That is one reason this book could easily be titled *Follow the Leader*.

Melissa's story was typical. She was a buyer for a large department store chain. After years as one of the store's most successful buyers she thought she deserved a shot at manage-ment. When she brought up the subject with her supervisors, they told her they thought she was such a great buyer, they would not consider moving her. At first she thought they kept her where she was because they didn't want to lose her services as a buyer, so she started looking around. After going on six interviews for management positions without getting one call-back, she decided to change her approach.

She sent me a personal consultation video. Apparently she wore almost everything she bought for the store. Her look could best be described as a fashion salad. She had a taste for everything. She did not have to buy another piece of clothing. I added nothing; I only took away.

She was a quick learner, and her instincts were excellent—the minute I described the look I was after, she had it. Two days after I put together a look for her, a new video showed up with her version of the look, which was better than mine.

A week after she adopted the conservative chic look one of her bosses said that she was glad she was finally getting serious about management. She knew the look was working because she had told her boss six months earlier that she would quit if she did not get into management. Her boss, like many people, believed what she saw, not what she heard.

Two months later, when Melissa was offered a management position by another store, her company topped the competing offer to keep her.

Another look that can be very attractive is what I call "dainty feminine." It is not nearly as effective as the healthy outdoor energetic look or conservative chic, but any woman who does look attractive by looking feminine and dainty should attempt it, particularly if she works with men. However, these women must dress in very conservative, traditional clothing. If a woman with a petite or fragile beauty dresses in very feminine clothing, she usually does not come off as effective.

Some women whose beauty is very feminine make the mistake of looking too cute. Mary, a manager in a communications company, explained that it is a look that makes men want to protect her. She could get almost anything from them. When I pointed out that the same men would not treat her as an equal, she agreed immediately. This look works until you want to move into management, then it hinders your progress. Feminine can work, but schoolgirlish does not. Your hair and makeup must say "adult."

Two years after Mary changed her look from cute feminine to serious feminine, she wrote to tell me that instead of being challenged every time she made a suggestion at the department head meetings, her ideas were being accepted without a fight. She added that if she had met me twenty years ago, she would be a vice president by now.

The sexy look, of course, is attractive—but should be relegated to social occasions outside the professional sphere. Dressing sexy at the office will give a woman a tremendous advantage with some men but will destroy her credibility with others—and turn off almost all women. If you decide, in spite of the research, that you are going to look sexy, you must be subtle. An obvious sexy look is usually seen as lower class and will destroy your credibility. While upper-class sexy may get you into the boardroom, lower-class sexy will at worst get you fired and at best keep you in low-level positions with little or no authority.

When we studied those whose looks were above average, average, below average, and far below average, no group had a tremendous advantage over any other. Each tended to test well in different areas. For example, the least attractive women were thought to be harder working, more diligent, and more dedicated to their jobs than were women who were average or above average looking. However, women who were above average looking were promoted more often and earned more than average-looking women, and average-looking women had a similar advantage over women who were considered less attractive.

Many of the women we questioned assumed that being attractive was most useful to those working as secretaries and receptionists, because men often hired women they could show off for those positions. That is not so—being attractive is equally important to all women. We showed videos of women in each group to over one thousand mostly male executives and asked them to pick the women who would fit in at corporate headquarters. Thirty-nine of forty-one women who had been described as attractive in an upper-class way were chosen by 90 percent of both male and female executives as suitable candidates for a top executive position. Among the fifty-seven women described as attractive, but who sent mixed class signals, only twenty were chosen by 90 percent of the same executives as having executive potential. And of the fourteen attractive women who sent lower-class signals, not one was chosen as executive material by a majority of either men or women.

The results indicate that being attractive works if you're attractive in an upper-middle-class way.

However, being attractive, even if you do not send upper-middle-class signals, does help. While average-looking upper-middle-class women were identified as executive material less than half as often as their attractive upper-middle-class sisters, they were four times as likely to be identified as executive material as their average blue-collar sisters. If you send blue-collar signals, being attractive becomes almost a prerequisite for upward mobility. While twenty out of fifty-seven attractive women who sent a combination of blue-collar and upper-class signals were identified as potential executive material, only three of fifty-three women with average looks were.

I am not suggesting that only attractive women make it into the executive suite, only that women whose looks are average or below average have to work a lot harder to get there.

When I first started researching this topic I used the phrase "strikingly beautiful" to describe the women whose beauty made it difficult for them to be taken seriously and the term "beautiful" for those whose physical appearance gave them an advantage in business. Once the research began it became evident that although physical beauty was a major component of being attractive, it was not the only component. A number of the women classified as attractive by the majority of those we interviewed did not have classic bone structure or a peaches-and-cream complexion. There is no doubt that beauty is only skin deep, but attractiveness is more than skin deep.

After reexamining the attractive women and running focus groups with them, we identified six different areas you can work on to make yourself more attractive. Body language, class mask (the way you hold your facial muscles), and weight affect your attractiveness as well as wardrobe, hairstyle, and makeup.

BODY LANGUAGE: POSTURE

The first and easiest step to make anyone more attractive is the development of good posture. Any woman who was not taught to carry herself with grace and style should practice by balancing a book on her head. Start by bracing yourself, West Point style, against a wall and placing a book on your head. Practice ten minutes every evening, walking from one end of a room to the other. After a week increase the time to a half hour. It is easy to do because by the end of a week most women can go about their normal activities balancing a book on their heads. The only precaution you must take is to remove breakable objects from the area in which you are practicing. When you have mastered walking, try sitting and watching television with a book on your head. I realize this exercise was last popular in nineteenth-century finishing schools, but it works better than any other method we tried.

A second exercise that will improve your posture is to pretend that someone is pulling a hair in the middle of your head up to the ceiling. If you try this, you will find yourself standing and sitting straighter. It is an old West Point trick, and it works.

The advantage to this method is that you can do it at any time. It works wonders if you do it every time you find yourself slouching.

CLASS MASK

The next step you can take on the road to becoming more attractive is to develop a pleasant facial expression. You may think changing the expression on your face is simple, but actually it is very difficult. If you naturally have a scowl on your face, you may need coaching. That is why I give seminars, do personal consultations, and have set up classes teaching this and other popularity skills. However, even those who need coaching most often make dramatic improvements as soon as they start working on their facial expression. It helps if you talk a friend, your mate, or a family member into being your coach.

Pay attention to how you hold your facial muscles when nothing special is going on. Unless you consciously attempt to change your look, you probably hold your face in much the same manner as your mother, your sisters, or your childhood friends. Since your facial expression is largely a product of your background, it is also an indicator of your background, and as a result, it adds or subtracts status.

I refer to the way people hold their facial expressions as the "class mask" because that is exactly what it is. It usually identifies your parents' class. Since most of the movers and shakers come from an upper-middle-class background, unless your facial expression indicates that you are one of them, they are less likely to find you attractive. In addition, upper-middle-class people are more comfortable associating with other upper-class people.

In order to change your facial expression, look in the mirror, but don't kid yourself that the person you see in the mirror every morning when you are putting on makeup is the woman who walks in your shoes or sits on your chair. Most of us—80 to 90 percent—have mirror masks. When we look in the mirror we stand up straighter and smile. Women who scowl all the time often smile, and those who have a wimpy look about them put on a high-authority expression. Many of us cannot face ourselves, so we lie to ourselves. The fact is, you can't work on the face in the mirror, you have to work on the face you present to the world. In order to find your real face you must arrange to have candid pictures taken. It is best if you can have someone videotape you while you are watching television, talking, eating, carrying on a normal conversation—that way you will get a realistic idea of how you normally carry your facial muscles. If you can't arrange that, still-camera shots will be almost as effective.

Once you determine how you look, you have to determine how you want to change. Most women, after looking at candid shots of themselves, decide they need to look more refined, in charge, or self-confident. Some women we coached found it helpful to role-play. They pretended in front of a mirror or videocamera that they were already a partner in, or the president of, the firm for ten or fifteen minutes every night.

Others found that simply thinking positive thoughts helped, and still others found that they needed the help of a friend to remind them when they were falling back into old habits. The most successful students were the ones who used all the methods. The habit you have of carrying your facial muscles is one that is firmly set, and it takes work to change it.

It also helps if you put several mirrors where you are going to be forced to look at yourself. Three favorite locations are across from you when you are eating, next to the television set, and in a hallway. The object of these mirrors is to help you monitor your body language and facial expression. It is only through constant monitoring and correction that you can change lifelong habits.

The women whose facial expressions tested best were those who looked upper middle class, pleasant, enthusiastic, friendly, and self-assured. The first two steps for most women is learning to hold their heads erect and learning to smile. Believe it or not, it takes physical effort to smile—it is easier to frown.

When you first start practicing to hold a pleasant smiling expression on your face, you will find that your facial muscles get tired. You have to exercise them by smiling. The more you smile, the easier it is to do. Some women said their facial muscles actually ached when they first tried to smile. They found it a tremendous effort, but the reward was tremendous as well.

As a general rule, if you look positive, if you look happy, if you smile rather than frown, if you look elegant rather than rough, the number of people who think you are attractive and able will almost double.

WEIGHT

There is no getting around it: thin is upper class, thin is beautiful, and thin is in. If you are even slightly overweight, some women will think of you as second-rate or out of control.

If you are markedly overweight, people will not think of

you as upper class unless every other signal about you sends an upper-class message, and you probably will not be thought of as attractive. The plain simple fact of life is that if you are overweight, you have to eat less and exercise more, and there is no easy way to manage this.

Research on diet and exercise indicates several facts that are undeniable. First, if you lose weight very rapidly, your chances of gaining it back are almost 100 percent. Second, if you lose it very slowly and attempt to change your lifestyle and eating habits, your chances improve only slightly. Third, if you don't keep it off for five years, it is not a permanent weight loss. Fourth, the only people who seem to have successful permanent weight loss are those who continue to exercise after they come off diets. Exercise appears to be the key to weight-loss maintenance. Fifth, maintaining your weight after you have lost it apparently is a far more difficult thing to do than losing it in the first place.

Women who are more than 15 percent overweight are less likely to be hired, be promoted, or move into management. It makes no difference what industry you are in or who your boss is, you are less likely to succeed. If you are overweight and work for a woman, particularly if she is into fitness, your chances of getting ahead are almost nil.

Iris, a bank officer, said she decided to lose weight when she and her mother were watching an old movie on TV, *The Keys of the Kingdom*. When the priest, who is the hero, tells a heavy woman parishioner to lose weight because the Pearly Gates may be narrow, her mother said, "So are the doors to the executive suite." Iris's mother had been the personal secretary to two presidents of the bank and noticed that not one new executive had been overweight. In addition, while some of the men had put on weight after becoming executives, not one woman had. Iris lost thirty-four pounds. She and every other woman we interviewed who went from being heavy to average said they were treated with more respect at work.

VERBAL PATTERNS

The way people see you is affected by what they hear from you. We researched over three hundred women and pinpointed these four areas in which they could improve their verbal patterns:

1. Pronunciation or accent
2. Vocabulary
3. Sentence structure
4. Verbal tone

We showed videos of twenty-six women coming from a variety of backgrounds to a cross section of both male and female executives and asked them whether the women were attractive. When we showed photographs of these women to a similar group, they had been identified as attractive. The only difference was that in the second test we had videotaped the women, and the respondents not only saw but heard them. In most cases the women said no more than one or two sentences. A typical example is, "My name is Mary Smith, I work as a manager for corporation X, and I am here to convince you our product or service is the best." Every woman with an upper-middle-class accent was once again identified as attractive, while less than half of the women who had an obvious lower-class accent were seen as attractive.

Mattie, a beautiful, sophisticated-looking honey blonde with a high-pitched voice and a Brooklyn accent elicited an unusual reaction. Everyone who saw the video snickered when we asked whether they thought she would fit into the executive suite. What made her so ineffective was she looked so upper class and elegant but sounded as if she were a waitress in a waterfront Brooklyn diner. The contrast between her look and her sound produced laughter.

A more typical example was Terry. She came from the Midwest and spoke middle American English. However, she obviously came from a working-class area of a large city because she "skid" talked. She occasionally dropped her *g*'s— said "goin' " instead of "going"—and gave mainly one-word answers. Less than 22 percent of those questioned thought she was attractive after they heard her speak.

The first thing you should do is record yourself when you are talking to your friends on the telephone and play it back. You may be surprised.

Look for three flaws: a strong regional accent or ethnic accent, lower-class speech patterns, or an unpleasant voice. You can rid yourself of regional or lower-class speech with the help of audiotapes or a speech coach. The best guarantee of getting a qualified coach is to hire a professor from a local university. The professor can also help if you have an unpleasant high-pitched or squeaky voice. If you have a high-pitched or squeaky voice, you must work at improving it because you will not be taken seriously or thought of as attractive.

However, the most accurate indicator of class is not accent, but vocabulary. The reason William F. Buckley sounds brighter than most commentators is that he uses a very extensive vocabulary. I have no doubt that Bill Buckley is a bright fellow, but he uses an extensive vocabulary because he comes from a privileged background.

There have been numerous studies on how people use language, and all agree that people from different backgrounds have a substantially different spoken or active vocabulary. Scholars may argue about the numbers, but nobody argues about the relationship. Most people who come from blue-collar backgrounds use as few as 450 words for 80 percent of everything they say. People from middle-class backgrounds use approximately 650 words to cover the same material, and people from upper-class backgrounds may use as many as 1,000 or 1,200 words.

In addition to the size of the vocabulary, the choice of vocabulary is also an indicator of background. If a person says, "The guy ain't got no class," it tells more about the speaker than the person about whom he is speaking. It says the speaker comes from a limited background and has a limited education. It also tells most people that nothing much has changed in his life. If, on the other hand, the speaker says, "The gentleman isn't very sophisticated," most people will assume the speaker is middle class.

Choice and size of a person's vocabulary affects what people think of her.

Increasing your vocabulary is not a very difficult undertaking. You can buy vocabulary enhancement tapes, if you wish; I find them very useful. I also suggest keeping a pad in front of the television when you watch the news. College professors are not the keepers of the linguistic flame in America. Standard English is determined by television anchorpeople. Therefore all you have to do is write down any word they use that you think could be useful to you in everyday speech. Write down not only the word, but the sentence or the phrase in which it was used. When you have ten words, put each of them in five sentences. Then tape-record yourself reading the sentences. Play this tape over and over, repeating each sentence or phrase. Never try to force a word into your conversation. If you play the tape often enough, new words will slip into your speech automatically. As soon as the words sound natural in your mouth, make another tape. It is important that they feel natural in your mouth because our students reported that when they spoke some words for the first time, they sounded wrong.

Newly spoken words, like new ideas, take some getting used to. Don't worry about it. You will gain over two hundred words a year if you do this exercise religiously. Since the difference between a blue-collar and middle-class spoken vocabulary is about two hundred, in less than a year you will change the sound of your ideas. People will think you are more intelligent, articulate, and attractive.

In addition to vocabulary, we are judged by our sentence structure. A professor of mine once said you can tell a person's background simply by asking her if she would like ice cream on a hot day. If she says, "Yeah," she is lower class; if she says, "Yes," she is middle class; if she says, "Yes, I would," she is upper middle class; if she says, "Yes, I would, thank you," she is upper class. He based his statement on the fact that people from poor backgrounds are largely nonverbal, and people from upper-class backgrounds tend to speak in complete sentences and are usually taught to be very polite.

If you simply make a conscious effort to speak in complete sentences or phrases, and to be as polite as possible, you will appear to be more sophisticated, intelligent, able, and attractive.

HAIR

Hair has been traditionally referred to as a woman's "crowning glory," and there is a good reason for this. A woman's hair has a major impact on the way people see her. Our original research showed that a businesswoman was most effective if her hair was shoulder length or shorter, manageable, but not so short as to look masculine. This remains unchanged.

A woman who wants to have long hair must put it up in a businesslike style. There are so many variations in hairstyles that I cannot recommend specific ones. However, most women, when shown pictures of hairstyles, immediately and accurately recognized which ones were businesslike and which ones were not. Therefore 95 percent of the time your guess will be accurate.

If you are not sure if your hairstyle is businesslike, assume it isn't and make it a step more conservative.

Long hair over your shoulders sends a sexual message to 10 to 15 percent of men. As a result, it makes you less effective in most business environments because it sets up an unprofessional relationship between you and these men. Hair that is too cute, too sexy, too young, too severe, too dated, or too disheveled does not work. I know that one popular style is to have a billion curls and let your hair flow all over the place. Another version of this style makes women look as if they just got out of bed. It works no better. The fact is, to most men this hairstyle looks as if it is out of control—the hairstyles that work best are those that look managed and controlled.

Finally, a woman's hairstyle can never send a masculine message—it turns off most men and a substantial percentage of women.

Most of the women we have run across in business do not

object to these restrictions. In fact, most have short, manageable hair not because they believed they were ineffective when their hair was longer, but because they understood that in order to be effective with long hair, they had to spend time every morning putting it up. Most of the successful women with shoulder-length or shorter hair said that when they left college, they had long hair. They had it restyled for convenience' sake. A number of women said that in their company long hair was the hallmark of a kid just out of college. It seems that almost all the women we surveyed wore their hair short by the time they hit thirty. One said it was almost an announcement to management that you are serious about your career.

If you decide your hairstyle needs changing, go to a top hairstylist and tell him or her exactly the look you are after. Most of the top executive women go to well-known hairstylists; they believe that these professionals have increased their attractiveness and effectiveness, and I agree.

When we sent women to top hairstylists, most returned with hairstyles that were attractive and, in most cases, effective.

Going to a top hairstylist is a little bit trickier than it sounds. If you call up a salon and ask to have your hair styled by Mr. Big, the person who answers the telephone will invariably try to steer you to one of Mr. Big's assistants. Mr. Big tries to save himself for his very important clients; he is a very busy man. The receptionist will insist that the assistant is well trained in Mr. Big's methods and that he will do a wonderful job. Sometimes that is true, sometimes it isn't. The one thing you can be sure of is that Mr. Big didn't get to be Mr. Big by being less talented than his assistants. Their next ploy is to tell you that to get an appointment with Mr. Big you will have to wait weeks or months or come in on a Wednesday morning at ten or some time that is equally inconvenient. It is worth the wait.

Once you have set up the appointment, tell them you don't want Mr. Big to be rushed, you want him to be able to take his time, and if necessary, you will pay extra for the privilege. This will let them know that you are serious about having your hair styled, and he won't come in and snip a few locks and then send an assistant. Make it very clear that you want him to do all the work.

When you come in for your appointment, come dressed in business attire even if the appointment is on a Saturday morning. The hairstylists I interviewed said that they look very carefully at the way a woman dresses because they understand two things: one, that a hairstyle should complement a woman's overall style; and two, that a woman's look tells more about what she wants than anything she says. Wear your most expensive suit and good jewelry.

Before you arrive, you should have a pretty good idea of what you want. The best way of determining this is to use the computer programs available in some salons. This will allow you to see yourself in a number of hairstyles. Make sure the computer program allows you to print out the results. Print out a half dozen flattering styles and test them. Don't show them to your family or your friends; they already have a mental picture of you in their minds. They are going to see you as most effective and most attractive in hairstyles similar to the one that you are now wearing. That is why you can't really judge your own hairstyle—you also are used to seeing yourself in a certain way, and you presume that look or a similar look is the real you. Find someone who can show the pictures to strangers. It would be helpful if the strangers came from the same socioeconomic and educational background as the people who are going to make critical decisions about your career. It would be even more helpful if they were in the same industry. If you arranged for another person to show these pictures to those attending a conference in your industry, it would be ideal. The easiest way to do this is to match hairstyles, test one against the other. Have them ask which hairstyle looks best on you and which one makes you look most like a competent professional. Pay no attention to your gut instinct; go with the research.

Take the pictures of the winning hairstyle with you when you go to meet Mr. (or Ms.) Big. Tell him about your research, and let him do his magic. Don't insult him by telling him to copy the picture. It is an engineering plan, and he will do the designing. A good hairstylist knows there are hundreds of variations on each style, and only a real artist can pick the right one for you.

I realize that not every woman is going to have the time to go through that computer program and have the testing done. It is useful, but not necessary. You can simply go to a top hairstylist and tell her exactly what you want. Most of them are well aware of the needs of businesswomen.

Whatever you do, don't go to the hairstylist and say "Do whatever you want," because she will. Remember, most of them are trendy, and the last thing any businesswoman needs is a trendy hairstyle.

In addition to leading the hairstylist in the right direction, you should also let her know your maintenance requirements. If you get up at 6:15 A.M. and have to be out of the house by 6:45 A.M. and on the train by 7:00 A.M., she will know that you need a low-maintenance hairstyle. When cutting your hair, she will take into account such factors as the natural direction of growth.

Remember, these are wonderfully talented people, but you must give them adequate information if they are going to do their job well. If you are lucky enough to get a really brilliant

HAIRSTYLES

TESTED
WELL
FOR THE
BUSINESS-
WOMAN

Wavy, not curly

*Shoulder length,
no longer*

*Short, not
masculine*

TESTED
POORLY
FOR THE
BUSINESS-
WOMAN

Too long

Too curly

stylist, you will leave with a hairstyle that is not only flattering, but effective.

Once you tell the hairstylist your requirements, you can't just sit in the chair and let him go wildly at you with scissors. If at any point he is cutting off too much or in the wrong place, stop him and ask him what he is doing. You must remain in control at all times because some hairstylists don't listen to their clients.

If you are among the fortunate who leave the salon with a hairstyle both flattering and effective, that is only step one. Have someone take your picture from the front, both sides, and the back, and put those pictures aside. Top hairstylists are so expensive that many women cannot afford to hire them on a regular basis, and when the women we used in this study went to another hairstylist, they found that the new one couldn't reproduce the cut. Having pictures helped.

Coloring Your Hair

I sit here with gray hair, thinking about coloring it. I have been offered a TV show, and one of the requirements is to color my hair. The producer said I would be more effective with dark hair. I know he is right—I have tested this premise. But I hesitate doing it because of the maintenance. One rule about coloring your hair is that unless you are going to maintain it, don't do it.

However, if I were a woman, I would have colored my hair twenty years ago. When a man's hair turns gray, there is good news and bad news. He is seen by some people as less effective and less energetic, while he is seen by others as more mature and reliable.

When a woman's hair turns gray, the news is all bad. She

is seen as old and over the hill by the majority of business-people.

The only other information is that while blondes may have more fun, brunettes are more successful. And redheads, for reasons I cannot even guess at, seem to be better saleswomen.

MAKEUP

Twenty years ago, when I did the original research on *The Woman's Dress for Success Book*, I said the best look for a businesswoman was as little makeup as possible.

The new research indicates that the best look for a woman is to apply makeup that makes her look as though she is not wearing makeup. Since looking young and attractive is absolutely critical for a woman's career, knowing how to apply makeup effectively is an essential business skill.

I have been researching makeup and hairstyles for almost twenty years. I first researched the subject when I was approached by two gentlemen who owned a series of salons and were interested in my going into business with them. I updated the research only twice, but I ran a number of small studies on this subject since. Before starting a new chapter, I surveyed 383 businesspeople and ran four focus groups.

Each of the focus groups were equally divided. One-third of the women were high-powered successful executives or professionals who used makeup well and thought of it as an essential business tool. The second one-third were women who applied makeup poorly, and the remaining third were cosmetologists.

I showed pictures of forty-one businesswomen wearing different styles of makeup to a cross section of businesspeople and asked them to comment. I then invited the focus groups to comment on the results. As a result of these discussions I concluded when a businesswoman applies makeup, her object should be to look upper class, energetic, and attractive.

If there is a key word to describe the style of makeup, it is "understated." The most essential characteristic of women who were thought of as most effective and most attractive was that they looked as if they weren't wearing makeup. The most successful women applied their makeup in such a way that you had to look carefully to realize they were wearing it.

Obviously you noticed if a woman was wearing lipstick, but the lipstick never made her lips voluptuous, too full, or sexy. In most cases it was used to give her face definition.

We asked the women to arrive at the focus group not wearing any makeup and to bring their makeup with them. Then we had each woman go before a mirror and apply her makeup. We asked them to spend about the same amount of time and go through the same routine they did every morning.

A number of things became evident. First, the attractive, successful upper-class women spent more time applying their makeup. They applied it more carefully. Their makeup was neater and more precise. Second, it was understated; it looked as natural as possible. Third, it was not an accident; they knew exactly what they were doing.

In these groups we had eighteen women who were identified as sophisticated, attractive, and successful. Eight of those eighteen women earlier in their careers had gone to a cosmetologist or an expert and asked for help achieving the look they were after. The other ten women learned to develop their look through trial and error.

Included in these groups were twelve women, with equally impressive academic credentials, whose makeup needed work.

They were not as successful as their more image-conscious sisters. Only one of those ever consulted with an expert on how to apply makeup, and she readily admitted that she didn't pay attention to what the expert told her. Successful women, like successful men, pay a great deal of attention to their image.

When I first faced the problem of teaching women how to apply makeup, I sent them to a cosmetologist. The results were disastrous. When I visited the salons I understood immediately what was wrong. The women working in the salons looked as if they had graduated from the Tammy Faye Bakker School of Cosmetology. Their own makeup was overstated, gaudy, and definitely lower class. One factor was obvious: Most of these women came from very limited backgrounds, and it affected how they applied their makeup and that of their customers.

After considerable searching, I found a woman who had worked for a cosmetics firm and gave instructions on how to apply makeup. She worked with me for two years. She met with each woman for ten to fifteen minutes. The women were delighted, and I was delighted with the results. A number of very talented women said her instruction changed their lives. Those in client corporations were keeping calendars and reported that they were treated better the minute their hairstyle and makeup changed.

While the men reacted positively to women who looked more attractive and energetic, their female bosses were twice as likely to react positively to the change. When we interviewed women in management positions, they said that a woman who didn't know how to put herself together wasn't very sophisticated, and they wouldn't consider her for a top job. For the men it was a subconscious reaction; for the women it was a conscious decision. So if you work for a boss who herself uses makeup in a sophisticated manner, she is not likely to promote you unless you do so as well.

Together we concluded that 65 percent of the women did not know how to wear makeup. Most of the women we dealt with were either executives or saleswomen. The vast majority were college graduates, and many of them had aspirations of becoming executives. They were twice as likely to dress well as to know how to apply makeup. Apparently dress is a much easier problem to solve than makeup.

Lipstick

Unusual or exotic colors did not work. No matter what color we tested, the softer and less dramatic the shade, the better it worked in business. Vibrant colors work only at night. During the day they say "lower class" on many women. Since the lipstick a woman chooses sends such a strong message, she must choose it carefully. It should be flattering and appropriate, but you do not have to limit yourself to one or two shades. We found as long as the lipstick complemented the wearer's skin tone, the shade she used made little difference.

All businesswomen should wear lipstick. We are so used to seeing women with lipstick that a woman without lipstick usually looks washed out. This is particularly true of women with fair skin and blond or very light brown hair. Petite and young women can wear more vibrant colors to draw attention without turning people off. Women with fair skin and light hair can also use vibrant shades of lipstick to give their faces definition, and women with thin lips can use vibrant shades to make their lips look fuller.

Nail Polish

The nail polishes that worked best were red and clear. Flesh tones and shades of peach and pink worked on women over thirty-five, but on younger women they often looked too frivolous. Black, yellow, and green, along with fifteen other unusual colors, identified the wearer as lower class, without power or education, and a lightweight, as did very long and hand-painted nails.

A number of the women we interviewed worked in human resources and hired secretaries and clerical people. Several of them said they regularly turned down young women—job applicants—because of their nails. When I asked the head of human resources in one company if she turned down applicants because of their nails, she answered yes, young men occasionally because their nails were dirty and young women just about as often because their nails were inappropriate. When I asked her to define "inappropriate" she said, "A candidate applying for a clerical position was turned down only if her nails were outrageous and a candidate applying for a position that required a degree and could lead into management if her nails or anything else were out of step." She reflected the views of the other successful women I interviewed.

If you have nails that chip and break all the time, you can wear fakes as long as you obey all the rules for real nails.

Eyeliner

Successful businesswomen do wear eyeliner. It must be subtle and carefully applied, and you should check it during the day.

I interviewed several women who had their eyeliner tattooed on. I do not recommend it. Makeup styles change, and it is possible you might be stuck with an outdated eyeliner. Theoretically it can be taken off by a doctor with a laser. However, one woman showed me that the procedure is not always successful. She managed to cover the botched job with makeup, but it was not easy.

Eyeshadow

Eyeshadows that work best are in natural skin tones. Try beige and earth tones that blend with your skin. Purple, yellow, green, blue, and similar colors do not work and should not be worn in traditional business settings. You can wear them if you are in a high-fashion industry or if you work for a woman who wears them.

Eyebrows

You can pluck, dye, and shape your eyebrows if it makes you look more attractive. However, if you end up with a pencil line instead of an eyebrow, it does not work.

Heavy Makeup

Wearing heavy makeup is advisable if a woman has a scar or similar blemish she wishes to cover up. There are makeups designed specifically for this. It is also appropriate for most women when they hit their late fifties or early sixties. Once a woman starts to look old, she loses some of her authority. Most of the time, when the fashion magazines picture a business-woman, they show a too thin twenty-six-year-old waving good-bye to her handsome husband and beautiful children. She is usually pictured running to work with one foot up in the air.

This unrealistic picture of a female executive has become part of our culture. I believe that is the reason so many women executives are forced to rely on heavy makeup and plastic surgery to maintain their effectiveness.

At least a dozen women in my phone tag team said they spend twice as much time getting ready in the morning than they did ten years earlier. They noticed when they started showing their age they were not taken as seriously as before. So they work at their looks.

Plastic Surgery

If it weren't for the fact that women who begin to look old are not taken seriously, I would never recommend plastic surgery. However, plastic surgery has become so common for executive and professional women in their fifties or early sixties that it seems to be almost a requirement. In addition, it works. Consider this: Fifty-three out of fifty-four executive and professional women who underwent successful plastic surgery reported a dramatic change in the way both men and women at work treated them.

Marilyn was passed over for vice president, though she was obviously the best qualified candidate. Out of desperation she tried plastic surgery as well as a number of other things and got the promotion a year later. The idea that a less talented woman had been promoted before her drove her crazy. Once she got to know the people who made the decision, she questioned them indirectly. She was told by one man that a couple of years back she seemed to have lost her edge, but everyone was delighted when she pulled herself together and was promoted.

She said she worked harder when she was competing for that opening into the executive ranks than she had ever worked in her life. She produced more, and she made millions of dollars for the company that it wouldn't have made without her. Yet all they saw was an old lady. She complained that men in their fifties looked terrific, but, she added, that was life.

Sarah, one of the most successful litigators in the country, said the minute she began to look her age, fifty-three, juries and judges didn't listen to her as carefully. She found herself slipping, and only through plastic surgery did she renew her career.

Julia, a manager in a large communications company, said that one day a vice president was showing a man in his early forties through her department. He went from one section head to another, introducing the gentleman, and when he was directly outside her office he stopped and introduced the gentleman to one of her assistants. When her assistant walked away the fellow asked, "Who runs this department?" The vice president pointed and said, "Her." The man responded, "Who, the old lady?" and the vice president said, "Yes." A few seconds later they walked in and said hello. She pretended her intercom hadn't been on and smiled, but she understood that she was in trouble. She took an extended vacation a month later and had a face lift. A year later she became the next senior manager. She is firmly convinced that if she hadn't had the face lift, they would have forced the "old lady" to retire.

If you decide that plastic surgery is an option that you want to consider, don't run out and have it done immediately. Your first step is to find the right plastic surgeon. Make sure the doctor is board certified. I spoke to dozens of executive women who were happy with their surgeons and a few who told me horror stories. You can't be too careful when choosing a plastic surgeon. Check the doctor's reputation and do not count on before and after pictures. Obviously a doctor isn't going to show you pictures of the women he has botched.

Mary-Ann, an attorney, said she checked to see if anyone was suing her plastic surgeon and found that nine women were suing him for mutilating them. She changed surgeons. She suggested checking with the local medical board to see if any charges are pending against the doctor.

The best and most comprehensive advice came from two female physicians in one of our focus groups. They recommended:

First, use a plastic surgeon that someone you know has used.

Second, go to a plastic surgeon in a major medical center.

Third, make sure your plastic surgeon is board certified.

Fourth, check on your plastic surgeon at the hospital where he works. If you have a family physician, ask him whom he would recommend.

In addition, if you know doctors or nurses who work in the community, ask them. If a doctor qualifies his recommendation in any way, look elsewhere. Nurses will be more forthcoming.

Five, hire a star. You will pay more, but it is worth it. Plastic surgeons are artists, and great artists have great reputations. One woman admitted that she worked with a doctor who was a prima donna. It was hard to get an appointment with him, but his work was wonderful and she would choose him over anyone else she knew.

The physicians' final piece of advice was to put off plastic surgery as long as possible. Apparently once you have your face lifted, it is only a matter of time before you must have it redone.

If you have your first face lift when you are age forty-eight, you may need a number of them before you reach retirement age. If you put it off until you are fifty-three, you are far better off, because each time it becomes more difficult.

At the end of each focus group we asked the women if they wanted to add anything. One woman stood up and made a statement that brought cheers from everyone at the table. She said that when she decided to have plastic surgery, a number of people who she thought would support her tried to discourage her.

She said, "I noticed something. Invariably people who tell you that you don't need plastic surgery, and that what you look like really isn't the central factor in your life or shouldn't be, are the same people who tell you that money doesn't count. They are either stupid or lying, so pay no attention to them."

I concur.

Chapter Eight

Casual Business Dress

The first time I used Dress for Success calendars was in the late 1970s. I gave calendars to fifty women in New York, Detroit, Chicago, and Boston. This was an extraordinarily gifted group of women. They had been identified by their companies as women who were headed for top management, at a time when very few women were considered for executive positions.

The study had two objectives: to see what very talented women actually wore to work, and to see if their choice of business clothing affected the way people treated them. The fashion industry at the time was claiming that if a woman reached a management position, she could ignore the dress rules because she had already "made it." Since there were a number of executive women who did break the Dress for Success rules, I wondered if they had a valid point.

The Dress for Success calendars were not very different from the ones I use today. The women were asked to record each morning a detailed description of what they were wearing and at the end of the day to answer questions about how they were treated by their superiors, co-workers, subordinates, clients, and support staff. The calendars showed that what they wore affected the way people treated them.

As a researcher, I was thrilled with the data gleaned from the original Dress for Success calendars. I was amazed at how much information they contained. Almost every time I went through them, I saw something new. They so fascinated me that three months after the study I took them to my summer house in the mountains. The office in my country place was so small that I piled the calendars on my desk, floor, and windowsills. As a result, my office was always cluttered. I hired a high school girl who lived down the road to straighten out my office twice a week. She was half file clerk and half housekeeper, and she usually did a very good job.

When I told her to straighten up the calendars, I wanted her to put them back in their original order. I assumed that she would put each woman's calendar back into chronological order and line them up alphabetically. When I came back several hours later, I was shocked to find she had lined all of them up according to date. She put all the January 1 pages together, followed by the January 2, and so forth. I couldn't really blame her because I hadn't given her specific instructions, so I decided to rearrange the calendars myself.

When I flipped through the pages, it struck me immediately that on days when these women were dressed casually their authority, professionalism, and competence was more likely to be challenged.

It was one of those rare and wonderful cases of research serendipity. Without realizing it, these talented women admitted something that they had previously denied when asked directly. When dressed more casually, they were not taken as seriously by other businesspeople. When I reexamined the calendars, I discovered that a substantial percentage of the challenges to their competence took place within five days after an off-site corporate meeting where informal dress was the rule.

The next study in this area was funded by the president of a large company who was thinking of changing his company's dress code. He wanted to know what effect having a casual dress code would have on his company. In an effort to find out, he enlisted the cooperation of several firms who had casual dress codes. He arranged for me to interview people working at those firms. I suggested that he line up an equal number of firms that had strict dress codes so I could compare results. Two weeks later I added companies with a third type of dress code. These firms insisted men dress formally but allowed women to dress any way they pleased. Then I looked at the salaries of women who had master's degrees, professional degrees, or five years of management experience. In companies with strict dress codes, these very able women earned almost one-third more than in companies where they were allowed to dress casually. Actually the women's salaries were lowest in companies where the men wore suits and the women dressed casually.

I have updated this study a dozen times, the last time in 1992. The gap between the salaries of women who dress formally and casually has narrowed, but only by 11 percent. The pay differential is now approximately 20 percent, with the advantage going to the more professionally dressed women. Further research shows that women who wish to make good money should work in a male-dominated field, for a male-dominated company that has a strict dress code.

The figures were so extraordinary that I at first questioned their validity. I thought if I found women who had worked in both types of companies, they would invalidate the original findings. After considerable searching, I found fifty-six women who had worked in both environments. I interviewed the women separately and ran two focus groups, one with eight and one with ten volunteers drawn from the fifty-six.

The first focus group was in New York and the second one in St. Louis. After just a few moments of discussion both groups agreed that in all the companies, including the most casual, there was a dress code of sorts for the men. They further agreed that if a man broke the dress code, he was called in and told about it, while in most cases the women were allowed to dress almost any way they wanted. They said that when they worked for companies that let women dress any way they wanted, not too much was expected of them. About a third of them believed companies with lax dress standards for women were making a statement that they didn't expect the women to perform at the same level as the men. They said that management in these companies didn't think women were as career minded or even working for the same reasons as men. They all understood that when the company arranged for the men to dress in suits and the women to dress casually, that put them at a tremendous disadvantage.

One of the women said that it wasn't a male chauvinist plot, that the women were responsible for the way they dressed. Clara, a vice president of an insurance company, said, "Don't be too sure." She went on to explain that ten years earlier she had been an assistant department head at the home office. When the department head resigned, the vice president in charge assigned her and a male assistant department head from Chicago to run the department jointly. After a few days she was delighted—he was helpful, cooperative, and charming. He regularly complimented her on her appearance, particularly on how she was dressed. The thought occurred to her that he could be conning her, but she dismissed it because he didn't overdo it, it was never sexual, and he never complimented her in front of third parties. She knew it was a contest, and she worked as hard as she could, but two months later he was made department head. After that he became a senior manager and then a vice president before she did. For seventeen years he remained one step ahead of her. She said she really didn't catch on until they met at a convention in Hawaii. He'd had a few too many of those drinks with umbrellas in them, the kind that don't taste as though they have alcohol in them but have quite a bit. So she asked him, "When we were competing for department head, did you compliment me because you thought it would give you an edge?" His answer was, "You bet, sweetie, and it worked. You were very good and had more time in management, and I was sure you were going to get the job." She said at first she was mad at him, then she became mad at herself.

There is no question that if a woman dresses casually and she is competing with a man or woman who dresses conservatively, she puts herself at a disadvantage. To research this we used pictures of men and women we described as "twins." They were identical except for normal gender differences: the man was taller, heavier, and so on. We put both in suits, the woman in a skirted suit and the man in a traditional men's suit. Then we showed the pictures to a cross section of business-people and asked which one was the vice president and which one was the assistant, which one was destined to go to the top, and similar questions. The men had a slight advantage. However, when we had both remove their jackets, the men won hands down every time. Between 80 and 90 percent of those questioned identified the man as the person with power and authority. When men dress casually and have to deal with relative strangers they lose some of their authority; when women do the same they lose most of theirs.

NEW WOMEN'S DRESS FOR SUCCESS

When I first started writing about the difficulties women have when they dress casually in a traditional business environment, I advised women against dressing casually on the job. Most businesses in the late 1970s had traditional, conservative dress codes; however, in the 1990s a large number of businesses have adopted casual days and some casual dress codes. It is not a male chauvinist trick, although if the world's most clever male chauvinist were to design a dress code to keep women out of power, he could not devise a more effective one.

Today casual days and casual dress codes can be found in many industries and all sections of the country. This represents a major problem for women.

Since a casual dress code will put you at a disadvantage, if your company floats the idea of adopting one, tell management that you are against it. The majority of women in companies where it has been adopted thought it was a wonderful idea when it was proposed. However, a year later most of those with executive ambitions have changed their minds. Many find themselves in a catch-22 situation. They would like their company to return to its old dress code but are embarrassed to say so, because they initially campaigned for the casual dress code.

The most common reason these women changed their minds was cost. Most women in management originally thought that a casual dress code for even one day would save them money, so they were surprised when they found themselves spending more initially. Our surveys confirmed this. However, we found that after three years women in clerical positions had spent a great deal less, while women in management and premanagement positions had spent just a bit less. There were four exceptions: older, short, heavy, or voluptuous women in management or professional positions. In what was often a futile search for suitable outfits, they spent small fortunes and complained bitterly about it.

Martha, a manager for a large manufacturing company in the Midwest, gave the best breakdown of cost. She was thirty-one, married for three years, and wanted to have two children before age thirty-five. She planned to move to suburbia and stay home until her youngest child was in the first grade. When I interviewed her, she and her husband were saving to buy a house before she took a leave from work, so she was on a very tight budget. Sixteen months before I interviewed Martha, her company instituted casual Fridays. On the first two casual Fridays in April, she wore outfits she owned but decided that she had to have at least three additional casual outfits. She ended up buying two additional spring outfits, three for the summer, and three that she could wear in both the fall and winter. While trying to save, she spent over $1,400. As far as she was concerned, she had to buy a second work wardrobe. Martha said she quickly realized that it was not like buying casual clothes for the weekend because as a manager she had to maintain a professional image. Her husband and the other men at the company just started wearing their golf outfits to work. Her husband wore slacks and a golf shirt in the spring and summer and added a sport jacket in the fall. In the winter he wore heavier slacks and a long-sleeve sport shirt with the same navy jacket, and so did most of the men in the office. She complained that men can wear the same outfit over and over while women feel they need to wear something new. Her complaint was typical.

The main reason women did not like casual dress codes was that they found they were not treated like professionals.

Iris articulated this dilemma best. She was an electrical engineer with two master's degrees, one from MIT and another from Columbia University. Iris worked as a consultant for a large computer company. Iris's company did not adopt a casual dress code, but she was promoted to a department where everyone dressed casually. She described her job as half research and development and half public relations. Her group customized software for large corporations. She explained that about one-fifth of the changes made in the original programs were unnecessary but were what the client wanted. Her primary job was to keep the client happy. Her biggest problem was to convince clients that she understood their needs sometimes better than they did. When she dealt with clients in the field, she had few problems. However, when clients visited her office where everyone dressed casually, she spent half her time defending the obvious.

The engineers in her department dressed in two styles: casual and crummy. Most of them wore sports shirts or golf shirts with slacks. A few wore short-sleeved dress shirts with hideous ties. The minute Iris arrived they told her the story of the engineer who showed up the first day wearing a tie. They snuck up behind him and cut it off. The rule, they explained, was that only senior engineers were allowed to wear ties, and most of them did not. She complained that she had to dress casually even though she knew she was not as effective with clients when she did. When I met her she was looking for the most effective casual wear she could find.

For the woman with executive or professional ambitions, casual dress days create an even greater problem. One of the questions women asked most was what to wear to social-business affairs, company outings, Christmas parties, and other informal gatherings. Before casual dress days came into vogue, women recognized that they lost authority when they left their business uniform at home. They wanted some direction. As a result of these inquiries, I researched the effects of wearing unsuitable outfits to these affairs. When I started, I assumed that it would have less effect on their careers than what they wore to work. After interviewing top-management people from a dozen companies, I realized I was mistaken. A number of the executives we questioned said that they used these affairs to appraise the up-and-coming young people in their companies.

The president of a Fortune 500 company admitted openly that he had a problem picking young people who would fit in at corporate headquarters. He explained that at one time he could accurately estimate how sophisticated a young person was by looking at the way she dressed. However, since you have them all dressing for success, their clothing is no longer an accurate indicator of their backgrounds, he said. Several of the young people he and his executives chose as their assistants lacked the necessary social skills to perform their jobs. Since these positions familiarized the young people with the way business was conducted at corporate headquarters, they were coveted and saved for future executives. After several disastrous choices, he started using corporate outings to look over the new crop of executive candidates. He and dozens of other managers said that when people dressed in casual wear they could tell which were socially sophisticated. It is very important because executive after executive told of young people whose lack of social graces embarrassed their bosses and the company.

Sophisticated businesspeople always knew these outings were places to be on their best behavior—that is why they referred to such gatherings as "dog and pony shows." The gatherings were usually dinner dances, office parties, and meetings at resorts. Using surveys, Dress for Success calendars, and focus groups, we came up with ten commandments and a few suggestions for selecting social-business outfits.

The ten commandments for choosing business-social outfits are as follows:

1. Your outfit should allow you to fit in with your peers. You should try not to dress in a way that separates you from your peers.

2. Your outfit should be appropriate for the occasion. If you are attending a formal dinner dance, you must wear a gown.

3. Your business-social wear should be as expensive as you can afford. If you shop for your business wardrobe in the best stores in town, purchase your business casual wear in the same type of store.

4. Your business-social wear must be upper middle class. This means that it must be in upper-middle-class colors, color combinations, and designs. Since women's leisure wear has so many variations and changes from season to season, if you were not brought up in a country club environment, you are likely to make mistakes. The best way to avoid this is to purchase traditional garments in the most conservative men's store in town that has a women's department.

5. Your outfit should be made of natural fibers—cotton, wool, silk, linen, and the like.

6. Your clothing should deemphasize your sex appeal. This can be difficult to achieve, even for the average woman, because the majority of women's leisure wear, particularly beach wear, is designed to be revealing. If you are very attractive or voluptuous, you are going to have to spend time and money finding outfits that downplay your sex appeal.

7. Dress more conservatively than at least half your peers.

8. Carry obviously expensive, traditional, businesslike accessories. They add status and authority.

9. Spend comparatively as much on your business leisure wear as you do on outfits you wear to work daily.

10. If you wear casual outfits to work every day, you should keep a jacket at the office. A jacket makes almost any outfit, including the most casual, more authoritative and businesslike. I suggest a navy blazer.

Remember that 80 percent of the time it is better to

- choose a traditional cut, color, and design of clothing.
- wear color combinations traditionally found in men's as well as women's sportswear—for example, a blue blouse with a beige skirt.
- avoid the latest fashion.
- avoid weird, even if it is the latest rage.

A few years back, looking like a tough biker was in vogue. Designers showed models wearing expensive black leather jackets and strands of metal chain. Harriet, a young, attractive professional working for one of America's giant communications firms, wore a version of that look to a company outing. She knew she had made a mistake ten minutes after she'd arrived at the picnic, so she left early. She worried that the outfit sent the message that she came from the wrong side of the tracks, but she assumed it would soon be forgotten.

I interviewed her ten months later . . . at her new company. She explained that as a result of that day she had two choices: to charge a half dozen men with sexual harassment or to leave. She said that the leather-and-chains outfit, which was no more revealing than those worn by half of the young women that day, convinced dozens of liberal and usually politically correct men—who themselves dressed stylishly—that she was "easy."

- choose dark colors. If your main garment is dark, you look more in charge.
- dress more formally than most of your peers without looking like an outsider.
- wear solids, not prints and patterns. If you must wear patterns, the best are small. Avoid traditional female patterns, such as floral prints.
- Do not wear flats if you are a women under five ten.

I never set out to develop general guidelines for casual business dress. They came about because I was queried frequently during the question-and-answer period with which I conclude all my talks and in my newspaper column. No one ever asked about general rules for casual dress, but most wanted to know how to dress for a particular occasion. For more than thirty years women have been asking me what they should wear to a variety of events.

The following section is based on the research I conducted to answer these questions. To keep the information current I conducted three focus groups composed of nine successful businesswomen who regularly attended business-social affairs. In addition, I questioned forty-one members of my telephone tag team, most of them two or three times.

THE BUSINESS LUNCH

Most successful businesswomen dress in the same style as they do in the office; 63 percent said they make no special effort to dress for lunch.

If you are a conservative, elegant dresser, you need not change. However, most businesswomen would be wise to wear an expensive and stylish version of their everyday office wear on those days when they know they are going to be having lunch with their bosses or important clients.

First, they *will* remember what you wear. When we asked both men and women to describe what their boss or client wore the last time they talked, they were far more accurate when they'd had lunch together.

Second, being well dressed will get you a better table at most restaurants, while a poor outfit may get you seated by the kitchen door. We questioned maître d's, and most admitted they decorated their rooms with stylish, attractive women, and even when they were not engaged in this practice they gave elegant women better tables.

THE BUSINESS-SOCIAL PARTY AFTER WORK

While it is advisable to dress stylishly on those days when you have an important lunch, it is critical that you dress in a way that will allow you to upgrade your look when you are attending an after work party. I recommend wearing a suit or dress that lends itself to dressy accessories. Most of the successful businesswomen we questioned said that to fit in with the male executives and their wives, they had to look sophisticated. About half of these women achieved a sophisticated look by wearing a stylish and expensive suit or dress to the office and, before going to the party, changing into a dressy blouse such as gold lamé, a gold or pearl necklace, gold earrings, and a small dressy handbag (black satin, for example). One-third of the women modified their business outfits to attend these parties but thought that gold lamé blouses and similar items were going too far. Most of these women changed their jewelry and purses. The remainder said that they kept their business image. While trying to fit in, they never wore anything to these parties they would not wear to the office.

Because there was no consensus among these successful women, I showed the same pictures we had used with the focus groups and the telephone tag team to male executives from the similar companies. I asked them to guess what position these women held, to estimate how good they were at their jobs, and to comment on whether they thought the women's outfits were appropriate for such a function. When they answered no to the last question I asked them how they would change it. More than 80 percent of those questioned thought the women who modified their business dress were the most successful and best at their jobs. They thought those who totally changed their look were overdoing it and those who wore everyday attire were not very sophisticated.

The successful women in the three focus groups, the telephone tag team, and the male executives did agree on several points. In the opinion of the majority, the most important thing to keep in mind when dressing for business-social affairs is that they are "dog and pony shows." You are there not to party, but to see and be seen. You should change your makeup, jewelry, handbag, and shoes (if they do not match your handbag). You can put on a different blouse, panty hose, and coat, but you should not put on a wild hairstyle, too much jewelry and make-up, long eyelashes, or anything that might be seen as cheap or sexy.

A BLACK-TIE AFFAIR

When the invitation says black tie, your host is indicating that he expects you to dress in traditional formal attire. While men have a uniform, women have options, but they are limited.

If you are invited to a black-tie dinner in a private home, a caftan or floor-length skirt with blouse is de rigueur. A floor-length black skirt with a dressy white blouse is a favorite of successful businesswomen because it never goes out of style and it travels so well. If the dinner is in a public place, an evening suit is by far the best outfit. The traditional model, with a floor-length skirt and matching jacket in an expensive and elegant material, is feminine, upper class, and, in a strange way, businesslike. When we showed pictures of business-women in a number of outfits suitable for a black-tie affair and asked if they were executives, those wearing evening suits were identified as executives 53 percent more often than women in any other outfit.

For a black-tie dance, the women's first choice was a full-length gown. The male executives thought that some of the gowns the women chose were too revealing. Both male and female executives said that dresses with dressy jackets or stoles were appropriate as long as the women did not remove the jackets. Ninety-six percent of the men and 77 percent of the women agreed that removing your jacket at a business-social affair was a mistake. If you choose to wear a gown with a dressy jacket to a black-tie dinner at a restaurant, you should keep your jacket on at all times.

A majority of all three groups thought outfits that were formal and conservative were best. The colors that tested best were medium to dark blue, black, and maroon, but suitable outfits were by no means limited to these colors. Most of the outfits I have described are rich by their nature.

This brings us to the rule that supersedes all the other rules. Formal wear must look rich and obviously expensive. Never attend one of these affairs in a garment that does not scream money.

THE COMPANY OUTING

Men have a uniform for company outings; it consists of slacks and a golf shirt. They wear it not only on the golf course, but to meetings. The best outfit for a woman to wear to a meeting is a preppie version of the same outfit. Do not purchase your outfit in the local pro shop—many of them stock only male outfits in women's sizes. Buy your conference outfits in a traditional men's store.

For most women the ideal meeting or golf outfit consists of a full skirt and a cotton blouse similar in style to the men's.

Check on the activities that have been scheduled for the meeting. You may need attire for a cocktail party, a dinner, or a dinner dance. Unfortunately the outfits in most resort shops are designed exclusively for vacation wear and are inappropriate for business-social gatherings. This is particularly true of resorts in the tropics. Most women are clever enough to purchase outfits needed for company social events at home, where they have a greater selection, better prices, and reliable tailoring.

What they often overlook are the sporting and outdoor activities that require special clothing. If your department is going to be playing another in softball, you may find you cannot get out of playing. To play softball you need footwear in which you can run, an action blouse, and pants designed not only to take rough treatment, but to deemphasize your feminine figure.

A number of women executives and professionals said that they refused to play softball or any other sports, because the men tried to treat them like helpless females. They thought it carried back to the office. Two women disagreed. One had five brothers and had learned to play baseball as a girl, and the other had picked up the rudiments of the game because she was a single mother and practiced catching and throwing with her eight-year-old son. Both said it would be wise to learn to play not only golf and tennis, but baseball as well. They said it helped them get along with the men in their organizations.

If you are voluptuous, you may have to choose other designs, because your main object should be to camouflage your feminine curves. In addition, you must wear a sports bra if you are participating in any activity that requires you to run or jump.

The one place the double standard is alive and well is at company outings. The classic example is the use of alcohol. A man can drink until he behaves badly, while a woman cannot look as if she is drinking too much. I have heard from dozens of women whose careers were destroyed, or at least sidelined, because word got around that they drank too much. One executive woman said that it was a rumor you could not defuse. If you continue to drink, people think you are confirming the rumor. If you abstain, they think you have a problem with alcohol. Most executive women recognize this and act accordingly.

We have also received many inquiries on how to dress when participating in recreational activities and researched that area as well. While golf is the sport of choice for most executives, some companies have their own sports—tennis, racquetball, boating, and so on. If you want to join the old boys on the field of sports, take lessons and practice. It is a worthwhile investment. Nine out of ten executive women said that if they had a daughter, they would advise her to learn to play a decent game of tennis and golf.

TENNIS

You no longer have to obey the white-only rule—the pros have made color acceptable in the best clubs in the world. However, if you are not sure, wear a white uniform with or without some splashes of color. One word of warning: Some of the pros wear peek-a-boo skirts that expose just a bit too much. Tennis skirts are short by nature, but they should be long enough to cover your derriere when you are playing.

GOLF

You not only have to learn to play a decent game of golf, you must know how to play the business game. In all three focus groups we had lively debates about whether a woman should ever let a man win. The consensus of opinion was that men threw games all the time to their bosses and clients. If losing on the green means winning in the boardroom, why not?

The basic golf outfits for women consists of a golf skirt and a blouse with an action back. If you feel more comfortable in pants, you may wear them, if you are not full figured and the pants are loose fitting. In addition, you need golf shoes, a golf hat, and golf gloves. On cool days men wear sweaters on the course. Most women are better off wearing a light nylon jacket.

Men wear the wildest colors and patterns when playing golf, for reasons I cannot even begin to explain. However, the same bright colors and wild patterns mark a woman as a duffer.

SKIING

You cannot wear those skintight outfits the Olympic skiers wear. If you are going skiing with business associates, you should wear a traditional ski outfit consisting of a jacket, pants, gloves, and a hat. If you are a beginner, rent your skis, boots, and poles at the ski resort and then sign up for lessons. It would also be wise to purchase your outfit at a ski shop. The most practical outfits allow you to remove the fleece lining and wear just the shell when it gets warm.

SWIMMING

Some bathing suits today are cut so a woman's derriere is exposed. You cannot wear these to a business outing. When I showed pictures of women in different bathing suits to both businessmen and -women, the women chose the more conservative models. While most men thought that a one-piece bathing suit was more appropriate than a two-piece model, they also thought a woman could wear a two-piece suit if she had a good figure.

Most of the executive women disagreed. They said that

women should wear only a conservative one-piece bathing suit at company outings. Seventy-six percent of the successful businesswomen said that if the top was too low or revealing, or the bottom too high, they would not wear that bathing suit to a company outing. A number of the women said they would not wear a bathing suit without a built-in bra. And some of the more voluptuous women said they wanted the bra to give more support than the average bathing suit bra.

Of course, whenever you go to a beach or pool area you must wear sandals and a cover-up over your suit. Not only is it in good taste, most good hotels require their guests to wear cover-ups when going to and from the pool. Bathing suit sets in traditional solid colors tested best, but any conservative bathing suit worn with a cover-up will work.

BOATING

For boating, wear Top-Sider deck shoes or sneakers with non-skid soles. I suggest you purchase those designed specifically to be worn on a boat. I was told by the president of a company about a young woman who wore sneakers with dark brown rubber soles. Every time she walked, she left a brown streak on the deck. Since it was his boat, he was not very happy. I am sure she was not invited again.

Almost any all cotton shirts and pants can be worn. However, since boating is a warm weather activity, summer colors are fine. You can wear denim, but you must make sure that your pants do not have the traditional studs, which can scratch the deck.

THE CLUB

Often the activities described will take place at a country club or yacht club. If you think you might be invited to take part in activities after tennis or golf, you must have appropriate clothing to wear. In most cases you can wear any outfit that would be appropriate for eating at the club where the activity takes place. Generally you should carry your gear in a sports bag and change at the club.

Keep in mind that even though the dress at most clubs is informal during the day, there are usually definite rules for dress in the evening. Since the rules change from club to club, if you are not sure, call the manager. Ask him if there is an official or unofficial dress code. He will be happy to help.

THE CASUAL WORKPLACE

Like it or not, want it or not, ready or not, casual dress codes have taken hold in the American business community. I estimate that from 60 to 70 percent of large and midsize firms have instituted a casual dress day or have a full-time casual dress code. This means that every businessperson, including those who work in companies with traditional dress codes, should have at least one casual business outfit in their wardrobes because they never can tell when they will have to meet with a casually dressed client. Of course, if you work in a casual environment, you must develop a business casual wardrobe. The ideal business casual wardrobe varies from one company to another, from one industry to another. Common sense and good taste are the only sure answers, but my research has turned up a few guidelines for different work environments. I hope you find them useful.

Blue-Collar Casual

If you work in a blue-collar environment where both men and women wear jeans or slacks or you must wear pants because you climb over, on, and under things, the best outfit consists of loose-fitting slacks and tops. If you are in management or hope to be, never wear blue jeans even if you work on a factory floor and everyone else wears them. Jeans send a series of negative messages. If possible, you should wear a tailored company smock or similar garment over your pants or keep one handy to put on when you have to deal with important people. The smock is needed to camouflage your feminine figure. Tailored tops that are designed to be worn outside your pants can be worn in even the most casual workplace.

Blue-collar men and women react best to women wearing traditional male colors. Blue-collar men do not respond seriously to women wearing feminine colors or prints. Solid blue, khaki, gray, and brown, along with half a dozen colors that can be found in traditional work outfits, tested best.

If you can wear a skirt or a dress, wear a conservative one. Blue-collar men react negatively to women wearing pants.

The Very Casual Office

In offices where not only your co-workers but your bosses dress very casually, wearing a jacket will announce to many that you are not a team player. Businesses, like all organizations, have official or unofficial uniforms. The easiest way to announce that you are joining any organization—IBM, Hell's

Angels, whatever—is to wear the organization's uniform. Conversely, not wearing the organization's uniform announces that you are not as committed to the organization as those who do. Dressing like everyone else is not simply showing that you are trying to fit in, it also announces that you are a loyal and committed member of the group. In spite of the advantages of wearing a jacket, breaking the dress code by putting one on is usually counterproductive.

If you adopt a conservative, authoritative, nonsexy, yet casual style and choose male colors whenever possible, you will have a definite advantage over the women in your office who do not. A number of women came to us in a panic when their companies went casual. After taking our advice, they reported that by being one of the few women in the offices who maintained their professional image, they had moved ahead of the competition. Even those who reported their offices were so casual that it was virtually impossible to maintain a professional image said knowing enough to dress for an important meeting gave them an edge.

While the average woman must dress conservatively for important meetings, petite, young, and attractive or voluptuous women who need jackets to look serious, nonsexual, and effective must wear them every day even if it separates them from the group. Nothing is worse than saying nonverbally that you are not serious or that you are primarily a sex object.

If you believe you are as effective as most of your co-workers when you dress casually, you should go along with your office's casual dress. You must keep in mind that the look you are after is not Saturday casual but business casual. The most common mistakes made by women in very casual work environments is that they choose outfits that are flattering or fashionable or dress as if they are not going to work. You should choose casual outfits that send a business message without separating you visually from your co-workers.

In 1990 we surveyed women in casual offices and found that 31 percent of the managers and professionals believed that once they traded the traditional jacket outfit for the more casual skirt or slacks outfit they found it more difficult to get certain things done. When we had women in sixteen companies with casual dress codes keep Dress for Success calendars that asked the same question, the percentage jumped to 46. I believe that the percentage who became less effective once they stopped wearing jackets was higher because from 10 to 15 percent of the women used the calendar to defend their casual dress code rather than to report data. This became clear when we saw how they answered the question, Did a superior, co-worker, or subordinate challenge your professional judgment today? Instead of answering yes or no, they made such comments as "The question should be, Did anyone successfully challenge your professional judgment today?" Or "That is none of your business." And "It does not make a difference whether anyone challenged me today but how I handled the challenge." These answers came from bright women who did not wish to face an unpleasant truth. Every time a businessperson's professional judgment is challenged they must put time and effort into answering that challenge, and if it happens more often than necessary it will negatively affect their performance.

Once we recognized the problem we set out to find a solution. After testing a variety of garments, we found that women were more effective when they wore a tailored top that hung below the waist or a loose-fitting vest that matched their skirt or slacks. In casual offices the unstructured smocks in traditional male colors and shirt jackets worked as well. You must keep in mind that when most successful men dress casually for work, they choose traditional garments because they believe that they look more effective. If you work with men and wish them to look upon you as a competent professional, you must do the same.

Seventy-four percent of the women identified by male executives as effective dressed in this style. Make sure your skirt is cut full and hangs at or below your knee, and in male colors, and you will fit in perfectly. Ironically, while dresses can work in a traditional office, wearing a dress in a casual office often creates a problem, because most casual dresses are ineffective. Sundresses, dresses with large floral patterns, or dresses in soft pastel colors are not recommended. Even in warm weather, dresses in summer colors did not test well. Neither did dresses or blouses with short sleeves or flimsy material.

The blouses that tested best in casual settings were man-tailored with traditional masculine shirt designs—solids, stripes, shadow plaids. The skirt colors that tested best were black, navy, beige with a gray tint, dark, medium, and light gray, taupe, and medium and dark brown, while the best blouse colors were white, light blue, navy, beige, tan, medium blue, ecru, and blue.

The more casual you become, the more traditional and conservative you must become if you wish to maintain a professional image. This is particularly true in offices where everyone dresses very casually every day. In such environments women operate at a tremendous disadvantage because most need the trappings of power and authority to compete with men on an equal footing. If the only signs of authority and power you can comfortably wear are masculine, you must wear them.

Conservative clothing is only one hallmark of an executive; there are others. A study we conducted in 1994 showed that other signals became increasingly important as clothing became more casual. We walked visiting businesspeople into a number of offices where everyone was dressed casually and asked them to pick out the executives. Most used the size and location of a person's desk or office as a barometer of her power. When the people were not at their desks they used hairstyle, makeup, and accessories as indicators. If you work in a casual environment, a conservative hairstyle and understated makeup will help convince strangers that you are an important person. Since a conservative hairstyle and simple makeup are not uncommon among women without power, accessories add status more effectively. Even if your clothing is casual, your accessories can be formal and expensive. Nothing dresses up a casual outfit better than a handbag, attaché case, watch, or scarf that costs a small fortune.

Twenty-two percent of the businessmen and -women we surveyed refused to guess unless we allowed them to talk to the people in the office. Since this is an unusually large percentage, we asked them why they were so insistent on this. The respondents explained that in their opinion the best, and in some cases the only, way to identify a person's rank when she is dressed casually is to hear her speak. They assumed that verbal patterns would separate the leaders from the followers. Obviously, if you work in a casual environment, your verbal patterns are very important.

A Typical Casual Office

In most offices casual dress has been defined or limited by edict or consensus—for example, no jeans, shorts, culottes, stretch pants, and so on. In a majority of these offices most of the men who have power already have a casual uniform: they wear traditional golf clothing. The closest equivalent for women is a traditional preppie casual found in the women's department of Brooks Brothers or similar stores.

In a typical casual office about half of the executives keep a jacket handy just in case someone important shows up. If you have a place to keep one, it is a wise move. In about one-third of so-called casual offices most of the executives wear jackets at least part of the time. If it would not look too formal, you should wear one as well. Two factors will affect your ability to wear a jacket on casual days: how formal your office is, and how you dress the rest of the time.

Janet was a classic example of how dressing formally during the rest of the week affected her image on casual Friday. She worked at an accounting firm in San Francisco where most of the women accountants wore suits or jackets when visiting clients' offices. Janet and her supervisor visited a client's office on alternating Fridays and worked there most of the day. Her supervisor was a very conservative woman who wore suits most of the time and very conservative jackets the rest. Janet wore livelier jackets and wore them more often. When the client instituted casual Fridays, they requested Janet and her supervisor dress casually when in their offices on Fridays. Janet kept getting requests to take off her jacket and join the program in spite of the fact that most of the men in the client's office wore jackets. She was forced to go casual even though she said it made her job more difficult. The same men who insisted she remove her jacket started fighting her recommendations. When Janet discovered that her supervisor wore jackets and no one said a word, she asked why. The client said that lively jackets were casual for her supervisor and that he didn't expect miracles.

There has to be a clear and obvious difference between your

regular work wardrobe and what you wear on casual Friday. If there is no discernible difference, you may not look as if you are joining the program. You should never wear the same look on casual Friday and another day; it will make you less effective on both occasions. Obviously, if you dress casually during the rest of the week, finding clothing that will make you look casual without destroying your professional image will be difficult. Conversely, if you dress conservatively during the remainder of the week, you can easily find casual outfits that work on Friday.

Skirts, blouses, and dresses in the same color and style work in most casual offices, as do the same hairstyles, makeup, and accessories. The only difference between a very casual office and a typical casual office is that in the latter you can wear a light or bright jacket or a vest.

Semicasual Offices

In these offices the men dress in conservative, traditional blue and gray suits from Monday to Thursday and in a conservative, traditional blue blazer and gray slacks on Friday. If you work in one of these offices or at the corporate headquarters of most large companies, relegate three or four of your more casual jacket outfits to Fridays. Nothing more need be done.

There are a number of companies where the male executives, in the European fashion, are now wearing conservative navy blazers, gray slacks, dress shirts, and traditional silk ties to work. They have gone international, not casual, so continue to dress in your normal fashion.

Mirroring

If you work for a woman, mirroring her image is even more important in a casual environment. We showed pictures of women working in casual settings to women executives and asked them to identify the least effective and the most effective. Sixty-three percent identified women who mirrored their style as most effective, and 81 percent identified as ineffective women dressed in a totally different style. Women whose dress indicated that they did not pay much attention to clothing were least likely to be affected by women mirroring their style, while fashionable women were most affected.

If you work for a woman who is much older than you, do not copy her style. Try to dress the way you think she would dress if she were your age.

Male Bosses

If you work for a man and you are not sure about an outfit, remember that for most men conservative and traditional are better.

The Casual Trap

The advocates of casual dress codes seem to have wrapped their cause in virtue. It is not uncommon to read that a company is instituting a casual dress code and how everybody is going to dress casually to help the Cancer Society or some similar institution. At first glance it seems that anyone opposed to a casual dress code is opposed to fighting cancer. Of course, that is nonsense. You can contribute to charity without adopting a casual dress code that will make it harder for women, minorities, and short men to succeed.

Unfortunately, what I call the "Mother Teresa" approach has stopped otherwise logical businesspeople from asking about the real effect of casual dress on companies and employees. A number of executives we talked to said they instituted a casual dress code because it would build cooperation and team spirit. However, not one came up with hard data to support that theory. I had a feeling that they were overstating the case, so when I was called on by companies to help them institute or fix their casual dress codes, I asked them if I could do follow-up studies on their long-term effects. Seven said yes.

At this point I do not have the full story, but I have a few insights. The claim that casual dress erases the lines between management and the employees, opens communication, and fosters cooperation is true only in blue-collar settings. In three factories we looked at, we found the workers had a more positive picture of management after a casual dress code was adopted. However, this did not offset the fact that women in factory management found it more difficult to give orders when dressed casually. It had become a major problem for women engineers in one plant where they had to gain the cooperation of men who in some instances knew more than they did. In a second plant two women had decided to continue to wear smocks that identified them as management even after their male counterparts stopped wearing them. I concluded that in factories casual dress benefited mainly the male managers.

A second claim made by advocates of casual dress codes is that they are an employee benefit because workers have to spend less on clothing for work. This argument has a great deal of validity. It does save most employees money. Most men find it cheaper to dress in slacks and a sport shirt or even slacks and a sports coat than in a suit. Most low-level clerical workers we interviewed said that it saved them money as well. The one group who reported that it cost them more money was women managers and women who were trying to become managers. They found they needed an entirely new wardrobe of business casual wear.

Another example of a half-truth used to support casual dress codes is that workers, particularly women, love casual offices. It is true that most women are in favor of casual dress when it is first proposed, but many change their minds when it becomes a reality and they see the effect it has on their careers and pocketbooks.

There are some who claim that casual dress increases productivity. The only numbers I saw indicated that any increase was short-term. When management pays attention to employees there is often a temporary increase in productivity, and I believe that is what is taking place here. Studies have also shown that if you convince people that anything—a casual dress code, a formal dress code, or having lunch an hour earlier or later—will make them more effective, they temporarily become more effective.

If management can turn a casual dress code into a company uniform everybody wears, including the top executives, that will have a positive effect on the corporate culture. If everyone wears jeans, including the president, it will open the lines of communication and make it possible for the company to react to change faster. The Japanese have known this for years; that is why they wear uniforms. However, that is not what is taking place. Casual dress codes bring down barriers only when they are first introduced. Within a year most of those in authority consciously or unconsciously begin to develop new work uniforms that identify their positions. If you go into one of these companies, at a glance almost everyone can tell who is in charge.

In companies where management is dominated by people from upper-middle-class backgrounds, the leaders wear upper-middle-class leisure wear. They purchase their business leisure wear in the same stores they purchased their suits or jacket outfits. Unfortunately upper-middle-class leisure wear is so different in color, design, and quality from blue-collar leisure wear that managers are visually more separated than they were when they dressed in standard business wear. In companies dominated by people from blue-collar backgrounds—such as high-tech firms—we found that those in charge usually carried or wore a sign of rank or position. In one high-tech firm the engineers carried green project folders, and in a construction firm the engineers and consultants from the home office wore distinctive hard hats. It reminds me of what happened when Chairman Mao made the officers in the Chinese army dress like the enlisted men. Within a year the officers were carrying pens in their pockets, the more pens the higher their rank.

Casual dress codes we studied have had the greatest effect on women, minorities, short men, and those who came from limited backgrounds. Each group reported after a year that they found it harder to be taken seriously. During one focus group I ran at a hotel, I asked an African American woman why. Instead of answering, she insisted I conduct a minitest on the spot. I had four members of the group—a white woman, a Hispanic woman, an African American man, and a white man—stand by the Coke machine and drink sodas. The group instructed them to act as if they did not know the other people. I then rounded up nineteen hotel employees and asked them to go into the hall and invite the executive to join us. Nine approached the white male who was not well dressed, four approached the Hispanic woman who was beautifully put together, and the remainder asked the executive to identify himself. If the world's cleverest male chauvinist developed a plan to stop the progress of women in business, he couldn't do much better than the new casual dress codes.

The only group that casual dress codes hurt more than women is women from limited backgrounds. Most people can tell something about a person's background just by looking at their clothing, because people from different socioeconomic backgrounds are attracted to different colors and shades of color. People from poor backgrounds are likely to think vibrant shades of color are more attractive than more subtle ones, while people from more affluent backgrounds are likely to think the opposite. There is nothing inherently lower class about vibrant colors. In the Middle Ages the rich wore vibrant colors and the poor wore muted shades. At the time, only the rich could afford to dye their clothing. Color is still connected with class. Today people from wealthy backgrounds are likely to mix blues and grays with earth tones, while people from poor backgrounds usually keep them separate. That is because those who buy in the best stores get materials that are subtly dyed, and those blues and browns go together. On the other hand, people who buy in inexpensive stores often get poorly dyed materials with harsh shades of blue and brown that do not go together. So good taste and conditioning will cause them to buy very different leisure wear. This means that women from privileged backgrounds will have a tremendous advantage. Corporate dress codes were great levelers. They put everyone in a similar look. Casual dress codes, as I pointed out earlier, have the opposite effect. They divide employees into the haves and have-nots. Without expert guidance, most women from unsophisticated backgrounds, without ever realizing it, eliminate themselves from consideration for executive positions. Socioeconomic nepotism is again becoming the most important factor in corporate success.

Casual dress days were not dreamed up by a male chauvinist or by a member of the privileged class. They originated in Hawaii. Some Hawaiians started wearing those traditional wild-patterned Hawaiian shirts on Fridays as a statement of ethnic pride. About twenty-five years ago high-tech companies run by men from blue-collar backgrounds put in casual dress codes that made them feel comfortable. The latest surge in casual dress codes is a product of an unnamed marketing genius at Levi-Straus who recognized that with the sixties generation coming to power, the trend toward casual dress was unstoppable and decided to cash in on it.

If the country's workplaces go casual, Levi-Straus will undoubtedly make money, but I doubt women will. Twenty-five years ago I conducted a survey that showed that women working for companies with conservative dress codes made more money than their sisters working for companies with casual dress codes. As a result of that survey I advised women to seek employment in conservative industries and conservative companies. I redid the survey five times, the last time in 1994. The results were always the same. Many women in high-fashion industries had fancier titles, but women in middle American companies made more. With that in mind, I continue to advise women to avoid industries and companies with casual dress codes.

The information in this chapter, as in the rest of the book, is based on research. For material covered in the rest of the book, the research was conducted over a period of years. However, 90 percent of the research on casual dress had been done in the last five years—and over half in the last year—because a revolution in business wear has taken place in the last three years.

It will help you to evaluate the advice given here if you have an understanding of how and why the research was conducted. At first I surveyed businesswomen and businessmen in client companies so I could answer questions in my column. Basically I asked questions to elicit two types of information from companies with casual dress codes. I asked the decision makers to describe what they and their people were wearing on casual days and what effect this attire had on performance, communication, and team spirit. As soon as I reviewed these surveys it became clear that few companies had well-defined casual dress codes. Most told their employees only what they could *not* wear. As a result, many were having difficulty putting together a casual business wardrobe.

In 1991 I was asked by companies to help them institute casual dress codes or to look at a casual dress code they had in place and make suggestions. This necessitated that I study employee attitudes and come up with specific suggestions on what employees in different companies should wear on casual days. To solve the second problem we ran picture-reaction surveys. This meant gathering pictures of people working in casual environments and asking various groups of respondents— such as buyers, clients, managers, and employees—to tell us what they did, how good they were at their jobs, if they had management potential, and so on. In the last three years we conducted nine surveys on casual business dress of the general business community and thirty-two of specific groups who were of interest to our clients. In addition, we had executives look over their own people and identify which in their opinion were dressing well, fairly well, and poorly.

Finally, in the last six months, we sent people into offices and had the managers comment on how their staff and people who visited their offices were dressed. Since our researchers were present they were able to ask followup questions, and as a result they uncovered some fascinating information. The first thing they noticed was that bosses, particularly women bosses, described heavy women's casual outfits in pejorative terms even when they were wearing the same outfits as their thinner sisters. When our researchers pointed this out, they said that heavy women should wear clothing that camouflaged their weight. When our researchers asked them if they could describe a casual outfit that would work for these women, most could not. That did not cause them to change their minds, however; they said it was not their problem. This means that many heavy women face an insoluble problem if they work in a casual office and cannot lose weight.

The same is true for women who are voluptuous or busty. A classic example of this was the liberated duo. Several years ago during a question-and-answer session after a speech, two women owners of an insurance agency attacked the very idea of dressing for success. Each stood up, gave a small speech, and walked out before I could comment. When I asked my host who they were, he laughed and said that they were known as the liberated duo and they attacked every male speaker. So the next year when they showed up for personal consultations I thought of it as a personal victory, even after they told me that although my information proved useful they were sure I was wrong about most things. I ran several seminars for that group; they attended each one and we sparred verbally. When one of my researchers asked them if they had changed their opinion of anyone in their office since they went casual, the first answered no. The second chimed in that that was not true. She admitted that they no longer send one young woman to meetings with important male clients. The woman was very busty, and since she started dressing casually they noticed the men were distracted by her. When I called them and asked if they realized what they were doing, they sheepishly admitted they did, and I won my first debate.

Their reaction, although out of step with their philosophy, was typical. My researchers asked 79 executives in companies with full-time casual dress codes for two years or more if someone in their company had been passed over for a promotion or another job because of how they dressed; 57 said yes and 7 admitted it was a factor. Even more significant, 42 of these 64 were women, and 36 admitted that if the office had a traditional dress code the person passed over might have been promoted. Many of the women we spoke to believed that casual dress gave them more choices. Unfortunately, one of those choices is to fail.

When we asked the decision makers in these companies to describe the dress of those who were passed over for promotions, they only described a handful as totally inappropriate dressers. They explained it was not that the women who were not promoted dressed terribly, it was just that they did not look professional. In fact, a few of the women were described by their male and female bosses as fairly good dressers. Their problem was that when dressed casually they were not the type of person who appeared ready to handle an important assignment. In traditional offices women fail because they do not achieve the look that everyone agrees says professional. In casual offices women fail because there is often no agreed-upon style that says professional.

We also discovered that if your boss is extremely neat *you* must be very neat, which is not easy in some casual outfits. This means that you must choose outfits that while casual do not wrinkle easily and are neat and crisp, not rumpled or look thrown together. Then make it a point to check yourself in a mirror several times during the day. Women who are by nature neat and orderly see precision as a virtue and lack of it a major flaw.

Remember that when executives institute casual dress codes, they change the rules of dress, not the rules of nature. When they tell you that you can wear anything you want to work, they are telling you that you will not be officially censured for dressing as you wish. They are not telling you that you will be treated as well when you dress casually as you were when you dressed in a more formal style. Even if they wished to enforce such a rule, it is not in their power. That is why casual dress is a *casual trap*.

COUNTERCASUAL

While the American business community has been going casual many serious career women have been moving in the other direction. Our latest survey of managers and executives shows that an increasing number of executive and professional women identify themselves as conservative dressers. Ironically, the greatest increase is in companies with casual Fridays or full-time casual dress. The women with whom we did follow-up telephone interviews indicated that when they were forced to dress casually they began to receive second-rate treatment. Many immediately started to dress as professionally as they could on casual days in hopes of reversing the situation. To their surprise, they were not only treated better than when their dress was casual, they were also treated better than their co-workers who continued to dress casually. These businesswomen are now dressing conservatively for the same reason men have dressed conservatively for decades: they think it gives them an edge. That is why casual dress can be a casual trap.

However, if you keep in mind that to win the image game all you have to do is dress better than your competition, a casual dress code need not be a trap. Remember, most people have no idea what to wear because no one told them. In good old traditional offices, people were told what to wear—suits, conservative dresses, and so forth. In casual companies the only thing people have been told is what not to wear—spandex, denim, and sexy anything. Some companies have not even done that. I am sure you can see that anyone who had a simple set of rules for casual business wear would have a tremendous advantage. That is why at the risk of repeating myself, I have created the following list:

1. Dress to fit in with your co-workers.

2. Be one of the more traditional and conservative dressers in your group.

3. Spend comparatively as much on your casual business wardrobe as you do on your traditional wardrobe. Buy your casual outfits in the best stores.

4. If your boss is a man, be as traditional as possible. If your boss is a woman, mirror her style without copying her outfits.

5. Wear only upper-middle-class colors and color combinations. If you come from a limited background, purchase entire outfits in the women's departments of the most traditional men's stores in town.

6. Stick to colors and color combinations found in traditional men's sportswear.

7. Carry and wear businesslike, statusy, traditional, and obviously expensive accessories.

8. If you come from an area with unfortunate verbal patterns, take speech lessons. We found the best teachers were college speech teachers.

9. Make sure that your makeup and hairstyle say "upper class" and "executive."

10. Wear nothing that might be considered too sexy for the office by your father.

11. On those days when you must wear a conservative suit to a meeting, when you are in the office replace your jacket with a loose-fitting sweater or casual vest.

12. The best business casual clothing is made of natural fibers—cotton, wool, silk, and the like. However, since you cannot wear anything that wrinkles easily and makes you look disheveled, choose natural fibers that have been woven or treated to resist wrinkling or blends that look like natural fibers.

13. Wear serious footwear—no boots, sneakers, sandals, spiked heels, or open-toed party pumps—and unless you are tall, don't wear flats.

14. Keep a navy jacket handy that you can throw on in case of an emergency.

15. Wear pants only if you need them to look like a member of the team or have to perform tasks that require them.

16. If you do wear pants, they must be tailored to deemphasize your feminine figure. A full-cut pair of slacks with pleats in a conservative color would be ideal.

17. Don't try to copy the outfits your male co-workers wear.

18. Neatness counts more when you are dressed casually. So check your clothing, hair, and makeup several times a day. (Most women, but not all, do this automatically.)

19. When dressed in nonstatus clothing, upper-middle-class posture becomes the primary nonverbal indicator of class and rank. If your posture is not perfect, practice sitting, standing, and walking with a book on your head. Suits camouflage imperfect posture; most casual outfits draw attention to it.

20. If you work for or with men, have a man check your casual business attire. If he tells you an outfit that you think is conservative is sexy or inappropriate, listen to him. Men see the world from an entirely different perspective.

21. If you cannot remember all these rules, remember that you will get by 90 percent of the time if your business casual look is *CUTE:*   Conservative

                                    Upper class

                                      Traditional . . . and like

                                      Everyone else's

The Dress for Success Calendar

If after reading this book you still have some lingering doubts about my advice on specific items or the entire concept of dressing for success, there is a simple way to resolve them. Keep a Dress for Success calendar.

You may be the exception to the rule, but before you bet your future on it I suggest you check. If you are testing a specific outfit, keep a record for at least twenty days. Try wearing the outfit you are testing and then wearing one I have recommended. If you are testing a style of dress, test it for at least a month in two seasons.

Whenever you are testing anything, your first job is to eliminate the variables. If you test a new expensive suit against an old worn dress, the fact that you received preferential treatment when wearing the suit would not mean you should wear suits. It could just as easily mean that you need new or more expensive outfits. If you are testing which style is most effective for you, keep the colors of the outfits the same, and if you are testing which colors are best, keep the style of the outfits the same. Obviously it would not be meaningful to test an inexpensive garment against an expensive one unless, of course, you are testing the effect of cost. If you use common sense, you will have few problems.

On the next page is a Dress for Success calendar. It is the one we give our clients. Think of it as a suggestion only, and change it to fit your needs.

If you decide to measure other areas, use the same 1 to 10 scale. It will let you more easily compare one score with another. However, when analyzing the results, assign an appropriate weight to each score. For example, if your clients are twice as important as your boss, double the value of their score.

SAMPLE DRESS FOR SUCCESS CALENDAR PAGE
Day/Month/Year

Outfit I wore today. _____

_____

How I was treated by: My boss	1 2 3 4 5 6 7 8 9 10
Others in power	1 2 3 4 5 6 7 8 9 10
Co-workers	1 2 3 4 5 6 7 8 9 10
Subordinates	1 2 3 4 5 6 7 8 9 10

Additional important people:

A) _____	1 2 3 4 5 6 7 8 9 10
B) _____	1 2 3 4 5 6 7 8 9 10
C) _____	1 2 3 4 5 6 7 8 9 10
My authority	1 2 3 4 5 6 7 8 9 10
My competence	1 2 3 4 5 6 7 8 9 10
My professionalism	1 2 3 4 5 6 7 8 9 10

Additional important characteristics:

A) _____	1 2 3 4 5 6 7 8 9 10
B) _____	1 2 3 4 5 6 7 8 9 10
C) _____	1 2 3 4 5 6 7 8 9 10

You can contact John Molloy at:

Molloy
P.O. Box 549
Nanuet, New York 10954

or

http://www.molloy-dfs.com/success/